DEAR FUTURE EXAM SUCCESS STORY

First of all, **THANK YOU** for purchasing Mometrix study materials!

Second, congratulations! You are one of the few determined test-takers who are committed to doing whatever it takes to excel on your exam. **You have come to the right place.** We developed these practice tests with one goal in mind: to deliver you the best possible approximation of the questions you will see on test day.

Standardized testing is one of the biggest obstacles on your road to success, which only increases the importance of doing well in the high-pressure, high-stakes environment of test day. Your results on this test could have a significant impact on your future, and these practice tests will give you the repetitions you need to build your familiarity and confidence with the test content and format to help you achieve your full potential on test day.

Your success is our success

We would love to hear from you! If you would like to share the story of your exam success or if you have any questions or comments in regard to our products, please contact us at **800-673-8175** or **support@mometrix.com**.

Thanks again for your business and we wish you continued success!

Sincerely,
The Mometrix Test Preparation Team

TABLE OF CONTENTS

Practice Test #1

1. Which of the following is NOT an ASCA Mindsets & Behaviors for Student Success domain?

a. Career
b. Academic
c. Social/emotional
d. College readiness

2. A known bully in the school is referred to your office. In addition to providing intervention for his violent behavior, what common issue or risk factor should you take into consideration?

a. Pathology
b. Potential to drop out of school
c. Future self-esteem issues
d. Poor conflict management skills

3. A school counselor is working with a student, Annie, whose anxiety about school performance has been interfering with her ability to function in the classroom. The counselor is applying cognitive behavioral techniques in individual counseling with the student. Which of the following represents an appropriate outcome goal for this scenario?

a. Annie will develop academic skills to use in the classroom.
b. Annie will learn to change her thinking and self-talk about school.
c. Annie will build trust with the counselor to talk about her struggles in school.
d. Annie will receive accommodations from her classroom teacher to support her.

4. What is one strategy a counselor can use to increase job experience and skills that would require community collaboration?

a. Creating an on-the-job training program
b. Finding part-time jobs for students
c. Offering more career-based or skill-improvement courses, such as auto shop and computer applications
d. Offering programs that focus on resume writing and interviewing skills

5. According to Jean Piaget's theory of cognitive development, the majority of middle school students are in which stage of development?

a. The sensorimotor stage
b. The preoperational stage
c. The concrete operational stage
d. The formal operational stage

6. Classroom guidance is most often considered to be which type of counseling activity?

a. Prevention
b. Intervention
c. Outreach
d. Academic

7. A student's standardized score report for academic assessment indicates that their stanine score is 8. Which of the following is a correct interpretation of this information?

a. The student's score is far below average.
b. The student's score is below average.
c. The student's score is average.
d. The student's score is above average.

8. According to the 2022 ASCA Ethical Standards for School Counselors, which of the following is NOT an ethical responsibility for school counselors conducting group work?

a. Arranging for booster sessions when necessary
b. Guaranteeing confidentiality among group members
c. Using outcomes data to measure progress
d. Informing parents of the student's participation

9. Mr. Lowe, a classroom teacher, meets with the school counselor to discuss a student, Erin. Erin has a diagnosis of generalized anxiety disorder (GAD), and Mr. Lowe is seeking information about how to help mitigate the impact of anxiety on Erin's classroom behavior. During their meeting, the counselor shares general information about GAD as well as common strategies and techniques that classroom teachers use to support students with this diagnosis. Their meeting could best be described as which of the following?

a. Consultation
b. Collaboration
c. Professional development
d. Referral

10. Carl Rogers' person-centered therapy identifies three key factors necessary for an effective helping relationship. Which of the following is NOT one of these key factors?

a. Congruence
b. Unconditional positive regard
c. Empathy
d. Transference

11. Grace is a high school student who asks her school counselor for support in choosing a career path. Using Frank Parsons' career counseling approach, what would be the first step Grace's counselor should take in beginning the career counseling process?

a. Having a conversation with Grace about her goals, interests, aspirations, and personality
b. Having Grace complete several tests in order to collect data about her personal traits
c. Having Grace research careers that interest her to identify possibilities
d. Having Grace complete the Self-Directed Search to determine her personality type

12. A school counselor is designing a mentoring program for students at school and is compiling information about school-based mentor programs to present to the principal. Based on available research, which of the following results would NOT be expected to be a possible outcome of a school-based mentoring program?

a. Increased executive functioning skills
b. Increased academic performance for mentees
c. Reduction of academic achievement gap
d. Reduction in truancy rates for mentees

13. Mr. Powell is a high school counselor in a rural area where families live up to an hour away from the school and many of his students are aspiring first-generation college students. He plans to host a FAFSA workshop prior to the upcoming submission deadline. Which strategy should Mr. Powell consider to encourage the MOST parent participation in his workshop?

a. Hold the FAFSA workshop during the school day for students to attend and provide copies of the slide show presentation for students to give to their parents
b. Post a link to the FAFSA application on the school website with a reminder about the upcoming deadline
c. Hold a FAFSA workshop in the evening and video record the instructional portion of the event for parents who can't attend in person
d. Utilize the school's student information system to send an email to parents reminding them of the deadline and directing them to the school website for the link

14. If a school counselor has a private practice, why would she refer a student in need of intensive counseling to someone else rather than seeing the client at her private practice?

a. She cannot see a client more than once a week.
b. She does not offer the counseling that this student needs.
c. She must have a full case load with her private practice.
d. She cannot use her position within the school to benefit her private practice.

15. Cultural identity is:

a. Primarily influenced by race and ethnicity
b. Fully developed by early adulthood
c. Stable across changing contexts
d. Dynamic and constantly evolving

16. A school counselor is planning a classroom guidance lesson on career development. Based on psychological career theory, what would be an appropriate first activity to include in this lesson?

a. Having students research careers they are already interested in
b. Having students complete a survey to determine their personality type
c. Taking a field trip to visit a real-life work setting
d. Having students research the skills and abilities needed for various careers

17. How are School Advisory Boards connected with parent collaboration?

a. They include the participation of parents and community in the decision-making process, which results in a feeling of ownership from these groups.
b. They are a way to get parents to volunteer and increase a school's parent participation rate.
c. Meetings are held at night so that working parents can attend.
d. They allow parents to see what is really going on with the school.

18. According to Piaget, what is a schema?

a. Information that has been taught
b. A universal view of the world
c. An individual's representation of something
d. The visualization of a concept

19. A counselor is a covered mental health provider under the Health Insurance Portability and Accountability Act of 1996 (HIPAA). As such, their clients have a right to:

a. Contest payment for services if records show that inadequate progress has been made
b. Request to have their protected electronic health records amended
c. Receive a copy of their diagnostic summary, treatment plan, and psychotherapy notes
d. Prevent the counselor from contacting family members in the event of a serious and imminent threat

20. Which component of a comprehensive school counseling program systematically provides a developmentally appropriate curriculum to all students?

a. Group counseling
b. Classroom guidance
c. Individual counseling
d. Individual student planning

21. Which of the following is true regarding the implementation of ASCA Mindsets and Behaviors for Student Success?

a. They replaced the previous academic, career, and social/emotional domains.
b. They differ at each school level (elementary, middle, and high school).
c. They are designed to be delivered through classroom guidance.
d. They can be aligned to school and district goals across domains and grade levels.

22. A school counselor begins at a new school and notices that there are few cultural diversity programs available. What might she do to increase cultural expression in the school?

a. Ask teachers to provide information on the ethnic demographics of their classes.
b. Encourage families to discuss cultural diversity at home.
c. Coordinate a field trip to a more diverse school.
d. Develop programs and events that celebrate and educate students about cultural diversity.

23. A school counselor is working as part of a team to evaluate a student for possible learning disabilities. Which of the following methods of data collection would be LEAST appropriate for gathering background information to support the team in selecting appropriate assessments and evaluating the student?

a. Collecting intervention data
b. Reviewing academic records
c. Surveying the student
d. Gathering a health history

24. School counselors at all levels incorporate career standards into their programming. Which of the following career-related activities would be MOST appropriate at the elementary level?

a. A career day during which students can learn about different kinds of careers
b. Mapping steps through high school graduation toward college and career goals
c. Taking aptitude or personality quizzes geared toward career choices
d. Researching a career of interest and creating a poster about that career

25. Which of the following is true regarding the rights of students and parents?

a. A counselor's primary obligation is to protect the student's right to confidentiality, but this right must be balanced with the parent's right to make decisions on their child's behalf.
b. A counselor's primary obligation is to protect the student's right to confidentiality, even if that is at odds with a parent's right to make decisions on their child's behalf.
c. A counselor's obligation to protect the student's right to confidentiality and the parent's right to make decisions on their child's behalf are equal.
d. A counselor's primary obligation is to protect the parent's right to make decisions on their child's behalf, as minor children do not have the right to confidentiality.

26. Conferences with parents and the school can come in many forms. What is one type of conference that will promote communication between parents and students, as well as the school?

a. Parent-teacher
b. Student led
c. Teacher-student
d. Counselor-student

27. A newly assigned school counselor would like to develop anti-bullying and anti-harassment services as part of a comprehensive school counseling program. The counselor's first step should be to:

a. Conduct a functional behavior assessment
b. Implement a schoolwide positive behavior plan
c. Provide stakeholders with a school climate survey
d. Develop a peer mediation program

28. Which of the following is NOT a necessary condition for a successful collaborative relationship?

a. Active listening, trust, and clear communication
b. Establishing norms and expectations
c. Having a shared vision and goal
d. Having a defined group leader

29. A school counselor learns during a parent conference regarding a child's attendance that the student's family was evicted from their apartment after the student's father lost his job. They have been living with a family member temporarily while the student's father continues to look for a new job. The family also faced the repossession of one of their vehicles, and the second vehicle is often used by the father while he applies for jobs. Which type of referral is most appropriate for the counselor to make in this situation?

a. The counselor does not need to make a referral because there is no abuse or neglect happening in this scenario and the student has adequate housing.
b. The counselor should refer the family to the county's housing services program to apply for a housing voucher.
c. The counselor should refer the family to the school's McKinney-Vento liaison for support, including transportation to school.
d. The counselor should refer the family to administration for an attendance plan because the child's transportation needs will continue to impact attendance.

30. Which of the following describes a classroom accommodation that is likely to be the most beneficial for a student who has difficulty seeing written content on the board?

a. Preferential seating
b. Extended time
c. Wearing glasses
d. Small group instruction

31. What is one of the primary reasons why counselors have a difficult time getting support from immigrant parents?

a. Immigrant parents do not challenge school authority.
b. Immigrant parents are often unfamiliar with American school systems.
c. Immigrant parents do not have time to talk with school counselors.
d. Immigrant parents have to work during the day.

32. A counselor wishing to increase students' ability to control feelings and understand their own feelings would develop what type of program?

a. Social literacy program
b. Cognitive literacy program
c. Emotional literacy program
d. Conflict resolution program

33. A counselor who assesses a student according to his or her microsystem, macrosystem, and exosystem will have a complete picture of the student's cultural and racial identity. What is this model called?

a. Systems model
b. Ecological model
c. Cultural assessment model
d. Full overview model

34. A test is considered standardized when certain components of the test and testing environment are the same among test-takers. In order for a test to be standardized, all of the following components are required to be the same EXCEPT:

a. The length of time given to take the test
b. The age of the individuals taking the test
c. The number of questions on the test
d. The instructions given when taking the test

35. According to the ASCA National Model, which of the following would be the most appropriate role for school counselors in dealing with bullying?

a. Issuing discipline for students who bully others
b. Changing schedules for students who are victims of bullying so they feel safe
c. Participating in the planning of a comprehensive, schoolwide anti-bullying program
d. Investigating complaints of bullying in order to recommend consequences

36. What type of students are developmental guidance programs designed for?

a. Those with developmental delays
b. Those with learning disabilities
c. All students
d. Those with emotional issues

37. Which of the following serves as the foundation for short- and long-term treatment plan goals?

a. The student's diagnosis
b. The student's desire to change
c. The student's insurance coverage
d. The student's collateral information

38. Which of the following is NOT a type of results report utilized by school counselors to evaluate the effectiveness of counseling programs?

a. Curriculum results report
b. Individual counseling results report
c. Small group results report
d. Closing-the-gap results report

39. Which of the following is NOT an appropriate strategy for facilitating course selections for middle-school students?

a. Calling a grade-level meeting to discuss course options and having all students fill out a course selection form individually
b. Holding individual meetings with students and their parents to discuss their course options and make selections
c. Incorporating course selections into a classroom guidance lesson and having students fill out a course selection form during the lesson
d. Using grades and standardized test data to assign students to courses based on current achievement

40. Mrs. Bell is a middle school counselor who is a part of her school's intervention team. The team is reviewing intervention data for a group of students who were retained in their previous grade and are completing their second year in the same grade placement. The team has determined that five students from this group need a tier II intervention. Which of the following describes an example of a tier II intervention?

a. Quality, research-based instruction provided in the regular classroom
b. Referring each of the five students for a special education evaluation
c. Classroom guidance lessons focused on student skills
d. Small group instruction focused on skill deficits

41. Which of the following program evaluation activities could NOT be conducted using data pulled from a school's student information system (SIS)?

a. Evaluate individual attendance data after completion of a small group focused on improving attendance.
b. Evaluate enrollment in advanced coursework by student subgroup as part of a closing-the-gap action plan.
c. Evaluate process data regarding the number of parents who participated in an informational meeting.
d. Evaluate discipline outcome data for a group of students who completed an anger management group.

42. When developing an intervention, a counselor should state the problem in a positive way. What is this known as?

a. Positive problem statements
b. Utilization
c. Reframing
d. Rephrasing

43. Which of the following ASCA reports includes a schedule for all classroom and group activities?

a. Classroom and Group Mindsets and Behaviors Action Plan
b. Annual Student Outcome Goal Plan
c. Annual Calendar
d. Closing-the-Gap Action Plan/Results Report

44. The DIRECT technique is a consulting method used in many school districts. What does DIRECT stand for?

a. District initiative regarding educational counseling techniques
b. Dynamic introspective reasoning for educational counseling theory
c. Direct individual response educational consulting technique
d. Direct individual reaction to educational counseling theories

45. Mrs. Simon is in her second session of individual counseling with a student who wishes to improve her grades. In their first session, the student identified her goal as completing her homework each night and turning it in each day without skipping any assignments; previously, the student had a very poor homework completion rate. Based on solution-focused brief counseling theory, which of the following would Mrs. Simon use to begin their second session?

a. Asking the student what challenges she faced in meeting her goal over the last week
b. Asking the student what is going better since they met last week
c. Asking the student what she was thinking as she completed her homework each night
d. Printing off the student's online grade book and highlighting missing assignments

46. A 7th-grade student takes a standardized achievement test in math and receives a score of "not proficient." All of the following are possible interpretations of the student's score, EXCEPT:

a. The student did not demonstrate mastery of established grade-level standards for math.
b. The student did not receive appropriate instruction in all of the grade-level standards for math.
c. The student demonstrated a lower level of intelligence than their same-grade peers.
d. The student demonstrated mastery of some grade-level standards for math, but not all.

47. A student comes into your office with a referral from her English teacher. This is typically a straight-A student; however, her grades have been slipping lately. She states that she has been "stressed out" but that nothing serious is going on. What issues would be the best to ask about first in order to determine the reason for her lower grades?

a. Self-esteem issues
b. Problems with peers
c. Difficulty level of her classes
d. Mental health history

48. Ms. McCoy is leading a counseling group for children whose parents are going through a divorce or separation. Which of the following would NOT be a goal of this type of support group?

a. Allowing children to share their feelings about their family situation
b. Allowing children to discuss the changes that are happening in their family
c. Allowing children to be reassured and feel hopeful about their situation
d. Allowing children to practice conflict resolution strategies and communication skills

49. Which of the following is a direct student service?

a. Consultation
b. Referral
c. Advisement
d. Collaboration

Refer to the following for question 50:

> Mrs. Tucker, a high school counselor, is evaluating various drug and alcohol prevention curricula for use in her classroom guidance lessons. As a part of this, she is planning a parent information night about drug and alcohol prevention. She is beginning her session with information about risk and protective factors for student drug use.

50. An effective, evidence-based program would be likely to include all of the following EXCEPT:

a. Student pledges or contracts to refrain from drug/alcohol use
b. Factual education about the risks and effects of drug/alcohol use
c. Strategies and skills for stress management
d. Focus on boosting protective factors

51. A school counselor conducted a small group focused on improving school attendance. In evaluating the effectiveness of the small group, which of the following types of data would be considered outcome data?

a. Meeting logs outlining student attendance at each small group meeting
b. The average daily attendance rate for participants at the conclusion of the group
c. Student post-tests from the conclusion of each group meeting
d. Student self-evaluations completed at the conclusion of the group

52. Which data type is reflected in the following example?

> *Fourteen sixth-graders received eight small group lessons on conflict resolution for eight weeks.*

a. Outcome data
b. Disaggregate data
c. Mindsets and Behaviors data
d. Participation data

53. Which of the following provides a three-letter career interest code that reflects a combination of personality types and work environments?

a. The National Career Clusters Framework
b. The Holland Code Assessment
c. The Employability Skills Framework
d. The Myers-Briggs Type Inventory

54. Mr. Scott is a new school counselor and is starting to collect data to plan his comprehensive school counseling program. Which of the following is a type of perception data that could be used to plan a new comprehensive school counseling program?

a. School data profile
b. Needs assessment
c. Pre-test data
d. Achievement testing data

55. Ms. Silver is a school counselor whose program focuses on helping students develop the foundational skills and mindsets to become lifelong learners. She does a great deal of prevention and early intervention work and helps students develop strong social/emotional skills. Ms. Silver's programming best aligns with the counselor's role at which level?

a. Elementary school
b. Middle school
c. High school
d. K-12

56. Which of the following is an appropriate use of intelligence assessments, such as the WISC, in a school setting?

a. As a component of a psycho-educational evaluation
b. As the sole determinant of eligibility for special education services
c. To guide students toward appropriate career paths
d. To make placement decisions for honors coursework

57. According to Bloom's taxonomy (original 1956 version), what is the highest level of learning?

a. Evaluation
b. Comprehension
c. Application
d. Knowledge

58. A 2nd-grade student recently mastered the skill of adding two-digit numbers. His teacher knows that, because of his mastery of addition, he is ready to learn the process of subtracting two-digit numbers with her support and guidance. The teacher is basing her understanding of the student's learning on which concept?

a. Assimilation and accommodation
b. Zone of proximal development
c. Social learning
d. Classical conditioning

59. The purpose of an interest inventory, such as the Strong Interest Inventory, is best described as which of the following?

a. To help an individual learn about how their personality impacts their interests
b. To help an individual match their interests with potential careers
c. To help an individual develop new interests, such as hobbies or activities
d. To help an individual understand how they relate to others

60. Which of the following topics or tasks would NOT be addressed in the group selection process for school-age children?

a. Informed consent
b. Voluntary participation
c. Parent permission
d. Allaying anxiety

61. A counselor finds that many of the parents of the students she works with do not speak English, and the counselor is not bilingual. What should the counselor do with regard to communication between the school and parents?

a. Send letters home and have the students translate them.
b. Do not communicate with the families.
c. Provide a translator for meetings.
d. Require the parents to take English courses.

62. When making a referral for a student's outside counseling needs, school counselors ensure all of the following EXCEPT:

a. The referral does not serve the counselor's personal interests.
b. The counselor matches the student with a district-vetted individual.
c. A collaborative relationship with outside providers is established.
d. A release of information is signed to protect confidentiality.

63. There are generally six levels of parent participation. Which of the following is NOT considered a level of parent participation?

a. Parenting
b. Communication
c. Continued education
d. Volunteering

64. Which of the following is true about the role of a School Counselor Performance Appraisal in an ASCA National Model program?

a. The School Counselor Performance Appraisal is not part of an ASCA National Model program, but is a licensure requirement in many states.
b. The School Counselor Performance Appraisal is a self-evaluation completed by the school counselor once a year.
c. The School Counselor Performance Appraisal is conducted by an administrator once a year using school, district, or state guidelines.
d. The School Counselor Performance Appraisal is based on an administrator's observations of the school counselor.

65. Which of the following is NOT an assumption of developmental career theories?

a. The career development process includes various stages.
b. The process of choosing a career culminates in early adulthood.
c. Career choices are reversible and made throughout one's life.
d. Career development is an ongoing or longitudinal process.

66. According to the ASCA National Model, which of the following tasks related to assisting students with post-secondary plans is an appropriate activity for a school counselor?

a. Calculating class rank and grade point average
b. Coordinating schoolwide SAT testing
c. Assisting students with understanding course selections
d. Copying records needed for college applications

Refer to the following for questions 67–69:

In survey-type assessments, a Likert-type scale is often used. For scales using an even number of responses, there is no neutral answer, and the individual must choose either a negative or a positive response. For scales using an odd number of responses, the individual has the opportunity to choose a neutral or undecided response.

67. As a counselor, you decide to use a 5-point Likert-type scale student survey to determine your students' knowledge and use of drugs and alcohol. What is one flaw of this method that you must be aware of?

a. Students might not understand the scale.
b. Students might choose the neutral selection to avoid committing to a positive or negative answer.
c. The method can produce unrealistic results due to social desirability factors.
d. None of the above

68. What is one downside to using a 4-point Likert-type scale?

a. It does not provide enough choices.
b. It forces a student to choose either positive or negatively.
c. Responses cannot be validated.
d. There is no downside.

69. A student is given a 5-point Likert-type scale and selects all neutral responses. What would a counselor determine from these results?

a. The student is laid-back and easygoing.
b. The student did not want to share his own thoughts and wanted to get the assessment done as quickly as possible.
c. The student did not understand the task.
d. The student is in need of intervention for indecisiveness.

70. Holland believed that a specific career will tend to attract people with similar personality types. One example would be the occupation of "teacher," which best aligns with which personality type?

a. Artistic
b. Conventional
c. Investigative
d. Social

71. In designing a comprehensive school counseling program, which of the following types of student development would NOT be a major focus of the guidance program?

a. Learning strategies
b. Self-management skills
c. Social skills
d. Emotional regulation skills

Refer to the following for question 72:

Ms. White, a high school counselor, is planning a small group focused on improving study skills. As part of the group, she has students complete an electronic survey describing their independent use of various study skills in the first group meeting, and she plans to have them complete another survey in the last group meeting. After a few group sessions, she notices that one group member continually asks other students if they are doing their homework, using their study skills, and focusing in class. This student reminds their peers that they are supposed to be doing their assignments and studying regularly.

72. Which group role is this student demonstrating?

a. Scapegoat
b. Gatekeeper
c. Energizer
d. Interrogator

73. ASCA's information-gathering tool for suicide concerns emphasizes all of the following components EXCEPT:

a. Directly asking the student about suicide
b. Asking the student about access to identified means
c. Providing a calm setting for a self-administered assessment
d. Engaging the student in safety planning with supportive individuals

Refer to the following for question 74:

A counselor begins seeing a student who has issues with low self-esteem. This student is of Chinese descent but was adopted by an African American family as a baby. The counselor knows that children begin understanding their cultural identities by the time they are three years old.

74. What responsibility does the counselor have toward the student regarding culture?

a. Provide the student with information on her Chinese heritage and encourage her to embrace it.
b. Suggest she join the Chinese American Club at school.
c. Question her feelings of being of Chinese descent but being raised in an African American home.
d. Respect the student's cultural identity as it is and assist her instead with the problems she brought to the attention of the counselor.

75. Alex is a middle school student who struggles with focus and attention in class. Alex's difficulties frequently result in incomplete work and poor grades on assessments. Alex's 504 team determined that he would benefit from preferential seating and extended time on assignments. Which of the following terms best describes preferential seating and extended time?

a. Intervention
b. Accommodation
c. Modification
d. Instruction

76. Which of the following examples represents an appropriate external referral that a school counselor might make?

a. A counselor refers a child with chronic absenteeism due to illness to the school nurse for assistance in developing a health plan.
b. A counselor refers a child with persistent academic difficulties to the school's intervention team for evaluation and support.
c. A counselor refers a child who expresses suicidal ideation to the school psychologist for evaluation of suicide risk.
d. A counselor refers a child who is struggling with significant anxiety for an entire school year for mental health counseling.

77. Which of the following is true regarding standardized test scores of students who are learning English as a second language?

a. If tests are translated into the students' native language, student scores are valid.
b. Student scores are likely to be invalid due to language and cultural differences.
c. Standardized test scores are a reliable measure of English proficiency.
d. Standardized test scores are invalid if the test is translated into another language.

78. Which of the following is NOT an appropriate method by which a school counselor would support students with disabilities under IDEA?

a. Providing classroom guidance curriculum to students with special needs as part of the full school program
b. Encouraging a student's parents to participate in a scheduled IEP meeting
c. Writing social-emotional goals for a student's IEP to be addressed through counseling
d. Providing short-term, goal-focused individual counseling as part of a student's IEP

79. A counselor initiating a school-family curriculum program will probably structure the program in what way?

a. Take-home activities for students and their parents
b. Group discussions
c. Surveys for parents
d. Counseling sessions for those in need of cultural diversity education

80. Ms. Gilmore is entering her second year as a high school counselor. During a collaborative meeting with her building principal to discuss the annual agreement for the upcoming school year, Ms. Gilmore reviews the tasks and activities that have been assigned to her. Which of the following activities would Ms. Gilmore advocate to have reassigned, as it is NOT appropriate for a school counselor?

a. Providing core classroom guidance curriculum
b. Counseling students about appropriate dress for school
c. Calculating grade point averages for students
d. Ensuring student records are maintained according to state and federal regulations

Answer Key and Explanations for Test #1

1. D: Only academic, career, and social/emotional domains are included in the ASCA Mindsets & Behaviors for Student Success. College readiness is a part of the Career domain; however, it is not the primary focus.

2. B: Bullies are at risk for a number of negative outcomes, including the increased potential to drop out of school. Counselors can implement many intervention strategies for bullying. School-wide interventions can include posted rules, announcements, and programs. Classroom interventions can involve the same intervention strategies as those implemented school wide, except on a smaller level. Individual interventions will address the student bully specifically. This type of intervention should be tailored to the individual and aim to define the root problem while providing education and intervention to change the negative behaviors. Referrals can also be made to anger management, communication, and conflict resolution programs.

3. B: Cognitive behavioral therapy focuses on changing thought patterns that contribute to undesired outcomes. In this case, the counselor wants to alter Annie's anxiety about school performance. While each of the other answer options may be a consideration depending on the scenario, none of them represent a cognitive behavioral approach.

4. A: Counselors can be responsible for more than just the mental and emotional well-being of students. When a school offers various career development programs, students who participate gain valuable skills for the future. On-the-job training programs are an excellent way to increase job skills. Additionally, these programs often help students decide what career path to follow. These programs allow students to go to school and work while earning school credits and gaining practical business experience. Counselors must understand that cooperation and communication with the community and leaders in the business community can be the key to success for these types of programs.

5. D: The formal operational stage typically includes children who are age 11 and older, therefore the majority of middle school students would be in this stage of development. The other stages represent ages 0-2 years (sensorimotor), 2-7 years (preoperational), and 7-11 years (concrete operational). Piaget's theory defines these four stages based on the linear development of logical concepts such as object permanence, symbolism, and conservation.

6. A: Generally speaking, classroom guidance is a preventative activity; it is systematically delivered to all students. Intervention activities take place when an issue or problem is identified, therefore an activity that is systematically delivered to all students is not an intervention activity. Outreach involves "reaching out" of the school and into the community, and classroom guidance does not fit this description. While classroom guidance may be focused on academic topics, "academic" is not a type of counseling activity.

7. D: Stanine measurements divide a standard bell curve into nine equal groups, and a stanine score places an individual score within one of those nine groups. A stanine score of 5 is the mean, or average, with stanine 1 being far below average and stanine 9 being far above average. Stanine scores allow an individual to interpret their score in relation to the rest of the group.

8. B: Section A.7 (h) of the 2022 ASCA Ethical Standards for School Counselors states that counselors must communicate "the aspiration of confidentiality as a group norm" but acknowledge limitations and understand that confidentiality cannot be guaranteed in small group settings. The

Standards also state that school counselors must arrange booster sessions (i.e., follow-up), use outcomes data to measure progress, and inform parents of the student's participation.

9. A: In this situation, the counselor is serving as the "resident expert" to provide information to the classroom teacher, who is seeking information to support his student. They are not working together to come up with a solution, which would be an example of collaboration; it is a one-way exchange of information. Consultation could be a method by which counselors provide professional development, such as by providing information to a large group of teachers. Although this consultation could result in an outside referral, as in choice D, consultation is the best description for the meeting itself in this scenario.

10. D: Carl Rogers' person-centered therapy, also known as client-centered therapy or nondirective counseling, focuses on three key factors: congruence, also known as genuineness or authenticity; unconditional positive regard, the concept of the therapist accepting the client no matter what they do; and empathy, or the therapist's ability to feel what the client is feeling. According to Rogers, if these three required conditions are met in an effective helping relationship, the client can develop positively. Transference describes the scenario in which a client projects their feelings or emotions onto the therapist.

11. B: Frank Parsons developed the trait-factor approach to career counseling. The trait-factor approach utilizes data from tests to match an individual with one best career. Therefore, a strictly trait-factor approach would begin with testing to determine Grace's traits. Trait-factor approaches do not rely on objective data from conversations. The Self-Directed Search from answer choice D refers to a tool used in John Holland's personality theory of career counseling.

12. A: According to ASCA, mentor programs benefit students in a variety of ways. Students who participate in a mentor program and are matched with trained mentors have been shown to have increased academic outcomes across subject areas; improved attendance; reduced truancy rates; and, for African American students specifically, there is data to support a reduction in the achievement gap for students who participate in a mentor program. While there is also data to support increased homework completion and improved class participation, improved executive functioning skills are not typically a product of a mentor program.

13. C: There are multiple factors to consider in this scenario to ensure students and parents have the level of support needed: the rural location, length of commute to the school, and lack of experience with college processes in both the students and parents. A live and recorded version of the workshop provides multiple pathways for parents, including working parents or those who live far from school, to access the instruction needed to complete the FAFSA. Choices B and D do not provide parents without college experience the support needed to complete the FAFSA successfully and choice A relies on students to relay complex information to their parents.

14. D: It is considered an unethical professional practice for a counselor to use the school as a place to gain private practice clients. While many issues can be resolved within the capacity of a school counseling program, there may be times when a counselor feels a student needs additional therapy or support. In these cases, the counselor should discuss these options with the student and the parents while keeping in mind rules of confidentiality. Additionally, after a referral is made, the school counselor does not have a right to information that the new counselor and student share. In certain circumstances, the school counselor may be asked to consult on various issues. If this occurs, the school counselor and the private practice professional must discuss the case only in factual, objective ways.

15. D: Cultural identity is dynamic and constantly evolving. Cultural identity is multifaceted and is impacted by race, ethnicity, gender, religion, spirituality, socioeconomic status, profession, and sexual orientation. One's cultural identity is a social construct and continues to be formed through social interactions and is impacted by historical and political contexts.

16. B: Psychological career theory, also known as personality career theory, focuses on an individual's personality type and the types of careers that best fit that personality type. A psychological or personality approach will always begin with a self-directed search to determine the individual's personality type. Researching careers that students are already interested in, or learning about the skills and abilities needed in those careers, are common activities in many schools, but these do not fit the psychological career theory whereby individuals are matched to potential careers based on their personality type. Before researching careers, students would need to take the personality survey to determine which types of careers are best suited for their personality type. A field trip to visit a real-life work setting would be more aligned with a social learning career theory, such as the approach developed by John Krumboltz. A social learning career theory is based on the concept that interests are learned, so exposure to a variety of careers and work sites gives an individual more learning and experiences from which to develop their interests.

17. A: School Advisory Boards consist of teachers, administrators, parents, and members of the business community. The makeup of this type of council is often directly related to the makeup of the school and the community at large. These boards discuss issues related to the general management of the school, along with district-wide policies and procedures. School Advisory Boards are responsible for developing school improvement and safety plans. These types of advisory boards are also responsible for delegating financial resources to various school programs. Parent involvement is necessary, as parents provide a voice for the parent community as a whole with students' best interests in mind.

18. C: As information is learned, individuals develop their own thoughts, beliefs, and representations about that information. These schemas are abstract and unique and assist the individual in understanding the world around them. Individuals also use schema to determine how they will act and respond to the world around them. For example, a common schema is how individuals perceive different cultures. Often in the form of stereotypes, these schemas are difficult to reverse once in place. Because of this, an individual with a negative schema about a certain type of ethnic group will react negatively to all individuals in that group.

19. B: HIPAA grants clients the right to request that a "covered entity" amend their electronic healthcare record. Professional counselors who use electronic health records to transmit health information in a transactional capacity (e.g., to bill insurance) qualify as a covered entity under HIPAA. Counselors have the right to deny the amendment if they determine that the client's healthcare record is accurate and complete. Payment for services must be agreed upon at the onset of treatment and cannot be contested based on the client's inadequate progress. Under HIPAA, clients may receive a copy of their records, including diagnostic summaries and treatment plans. However, psychotherapy notes are considered to be an exemption. Psychotherapy notes are a counselor's personal notes and are typically not a part of the client's medical record. When the client poses a serious and imminent threat to themselves or others, counselors can contact family members without client authorization.

20. B: Classroom guidance is the only component that fits the criteria described in the question. All students benefit from the developmentally appropriate curriculum provided by the school counselor during classroom guidance lessons. In fact, this systematic method of reaching all students is one of the main benefits of providing a classroom guidance curriculum. For ASCA

Mindsets and Behaviors, which all students are expected to demonstrate mastery of, classroom guidance provides a method to reach each student.

21. D: The ASCA Mindsets and Behaviors for Student Success represent the attitudes and behaviors essential for student success and can be applied to the academic, career, and social/emotional domains across grade levels. The Mindsets and Behaviors can be taught through all direct services, including classroom guidance, small group counseling, and individual counseling.

22. D: Education is the key to increasing tolerance and understanding between various cultures. Developing educational programs for students as well as teachers can offer a venue for these individuals to ask questions and gain a clear understanding of cultural diversity. It is also an opportunity to eliminate negative stereotypes. Additionally, offering programs or opportunities for students to celebrate their cultures will serve to provide education about other cultures to students from all backgrounds. These opportunities can be as simple as announcing various holidays celebrated by the different cultures in the school or allowing students to display pictures or information about their cultures in the halls of the school.

23. C: Evaluating a student for a learning disability requires a review of a variety of existing data from a variety of sources. In addition, reviewing this data can be useful in selecting appropriate assessments for the student. For example, if a review of the child's academic record indicates a consistent difficulty in mathematics, then there is a reason to assess the child for a learning disability in mathematics. The review of existing data must be based on objective information and measurable objectives, so surveying the student would be the least appropriate.

24. A: Career counseling at the elementary level primarily focuses on exposing students to various career options and career clusters. More focused planning and research would be more appropriate at the secondary level.

25. A: According to the ASCA Ethical Standards for School Counselors, a counselor's primary obligation is to protect the student's right to confidentiality. The Ethical Standards indicate that the counselor should balance this right with an understanding of the rights of parents to be "the guiding voice in their children's lives." Particularly when there is a risk of serious and foreseeable harm to the student, a student's right to confidentiality may need to be breached to prevent such harm and protect the rights of the parents.

26. B: A student-led conference is one in which the student participates in the preparation and presentation of the conference. This is a good strategy to encourage student-parent communication. This is also a good strategy to use to show parents the capabilities of their children. Student-led conferences offer students a number of advantages. By preparing a presentation for the conference, the student develops a sense of ownership. Additionally, this strategy holds the student accountable for schoolwork that is presented during the meeting. Finally, this type of conference gives the student the opportunity to improve on oral and visual presentation skills in a nonthreatening environment.

27. C: Providing stakeholders with a school climate survey is the first step in developing anti-bullying and anti-harassment strategies as part of a comprehensive school counseling program. ASCA recognizes the importance of promoting safe schools based on data-informed decision-making. A positive school climate is one in which students feel secure and free from bullying, discrimination, and harassment. Functional behavior assessments are conducted on individuals to determine the nature of chronic problematic behavior. Implementation of a schoolwide positive behavior plan would first require support from stakeholders. Developing a peer mediation program would be most effective with school and community support.

28. D: Having a specific group leader is not necessary for a successful collaborative relationship. In fact, leaderless collaboration happens frequently in schools. Trust, openness, clear communication, and active listening are all necessary conditions for successful collaboration. In addition, an effective collaborative team has established norms, expectations, and a shared vision or goal. School counselors can be an asset to many collaborative teams because they are skilled in communication and active listening and can help foster trust and respect among team members.

29. C: The McKinney-Vento Homeless Assistance Act includes families who are "doubled up," meaning living with other families or sharing housing due to loss of permanent housing, in the definition for "homeless." While these situations are often temporary, students who face housing insecurity often require additional support to ensure they are able to be successful in school. Once a child or family is referred to the school's McKinney-Vento liaison and qualified under that act, the liaison coordinates support as needed with other departments and staff members, including transportation, attendance, and providing information about housing programs. The student described in the scenario may need support with transportation, flexible attendance policies, or other supports, but the counselor should refer the child's case to the McKinney-Vento liaison first in order to establish a qualifying situation for those supports. Lack of stable housing is not the same as abuse or neglect.

30. A: Preferential seating is a classroom accommodation that allows for a child to be seated in an area of the classroom that best addresses their needs; in this case, preferential seating may include the child sitting near the board for the best chance at seeing what is written. Extended time is a classroom accommodation, but the connection between difficulty seeing what is written on the board and providing extended time is not clear. Wearing glasses would probably help, but this does not describe a classroom accommodation, as glasses are not provided in the classroom. Cues or reminders to wear prescription glasses may be a good strategy for the student described, but only if forgetting to wear glasses is an issue. Finally, small group instruction describes an intervention or instructional strategy, not a classroom accommodation. In addition, the link between not being able to see the board and small group instruction is not very clear.

31. B: Immigrant parents have many challenges when sending their children to school in America. Often, the parents do not speak English and are unfamiliar with the American school system. While language barriers often result in parents not participating in their children's education, a counselor can easily offer translators and other educational opportunities to overcome these barriers. However, if parents continue to be unclear about the needs and expectations of the school system, immigrant parents will continue to be inactive. This can be overcome by providing a supportive environment for both the parents and the students. Counselors in school systems with a high immigrant population will need to serve as "school-home-community liaisons" in order to promote the needs of the students and their families.

32. C: Emotional literacy is also referred to as intrapersonal skills. Individuals with good intrapersonal skills are aware of their own feelings and have an understanding of how these emotions affect their actions. This understanding helps individuals cope with emotional personal situations as well as display empathy for others. Additionally, understanding emotions also helps students manage and control their emotions. This type of program also helps students understand the importance and value of teamwork and cooperation with others. Developing a program that addresses intrapersonal skills serves to increase students' self-awareness and self-esteem.

33. B: The ecological model consists of the microsystem, macrosystem, and exosystem. The microsystem encompasses the student's immediate family and support systems. This will include parents, siblings, extended family, and friends. The macrosystem is defined by the student's culture. This will vary from student to student and often may include various subcultures. The exosystem refers to the student's social support systems, such as their community. Understanding these three aspects of a student's support systems will assist in developing appropriate programs and interventions, as the counselor will be able to incorporate the student's beliefs, morals, and values into counseling programs.

34. B: For a test to be standardized, the test questions, instructions, and testing procedures need to be consistent. Educators who administer standardized tests such as the SAT or end-of-grade tests are likely familiar with the requirements to read instructions from a script, carefully time the test administration, and maintain the consistency of the test format among test-takers. The age of the test-takers, however, has no impact on the standardization of the test itself. For example, many younger students take the SAT as part of gifted education programs or for practice for the future. If standardized test results are norm-referenced, the ages of test-takers could affect the norming group, but they do not affect the standardization of the test itself.

35. C: According to the ASCA National Model, it is not appropriate for school counselors to be a part of issuing student discipline or be responsible for clerical tasks such as schedule changes. School counselors are an appropriate member of a team responsible for planning a comprehensive, schoolwide anti-bullying program.

36. C: Developmental guidance programs are geared toward all students. These programs focus on understanding and assisting the students with their academic needs by offering services such as tutoring or peer mentoring. In order to meet the social needs of students, developmental programs embrace the cultural identities of students and aim to provide programs, increase student support systems, and offer opportunities for students to express their individuality. This type of program will also enhance students' cognitive development and provide opportunities to increase their understanding of themselves and the world around them. Because programs developed as part of a comprehensive developmental guidance program offer positive opportunities for growth and development, they are appropriate for all students.

37. A: The client's diagnosis serves as the foundation for treatment goals. The assessment, diagnosis, and case conceptualization should form the basis for a client's treatment plan. Treatment planning is a collaborative effort between the client and counselor, naturally incorporating a client's desire to change. The number of sessions may be influenced by insurance coverage; however, the goals themselves do not rely on that information. Collateral information is part of the assessment process rather than treatment planning.

38. B: An individual counseling results report is not an actual report used by school counselors. Each of the other major components of a school counseling program is evaluated with a results report that corresponds with the action plan created for that component. A curriculum action plan is evaluated with a curriculum results report, a small group action plan is evaluated with a small group results report, and a closing-the-gap action plan is evaluated with a closing-the-gap results report. Each of these results reports includes process, perception, and outcome data in order to evaluate program components.

39. D: ASCA has a variety of position statements that touch on academic topics, including course selection. A school counselor should use a variety of data sources when assisting with student academic planning, so using grades and standardized test data alone is not an appropriate strategy.

Many school counselors may find themselves in the position where their school or district policy requires course selections to be based on grades and test scores, and in those situations, the counselor would act as an advocate for systemic change. A comprehensive school counseling program will likely use multiple strategies for facilitating course selections at any level. Grade-level meetings and/or classroom guidance lessons are very common ways to facilitate the course selection process, but counselors should keep in mind their students' background knowledge and comfort with the course selection process when opting for these strategies. In addition, students may have individual needs or specific questions that would be missed in these whole-group formats. Depending on the counselor's caseload, having individual meetings with each student and their parents may not be feasible, but there are usually individual students for whom this is appropriate.

40. D: A tier II intervention is typically a small, group-level intervention for those students who have demonstrated a need for a higher level of support. These are intermediate-level interventions between tier I (whole-class or whole-school instructional practices) and tier III (individualized, intensive interventions). Therefore, small group instruction is the only choice that represents an intermediate, small group level intervention.

41. C: The student information system (SIS) is a very important resource for data-driven school counselors. Many data points essential to program evaluation activities can be found within this system, including individual, subgroup, and schoolwide data. Outcome data, in particular, is usually found within the SIS, including attendance rates, promotion and retention rates, graduation rates, student grade point averages, discipline referrals, suspensions, test scores, and so on. Process data, such as the information described in answer choice C, and perception data are typically harder to pull from the SIS and are more likely to be found in surveys, pre- and post-tests, sign-in sheets, needs assessments, and so forth. Each of these types of data is essential to a comprehensive program evaluation.

42. C: Reframing is the restatement of a problem or issue in a positive light. This is the first step when developing an intervention for solution-focused brief counseling. Utilization is the second step in this process. Utilization involves taking a student's values and belief system into consideration. Also at this stage, the counselor must consider the student's motivations in applying the intervention. This information will be gathered from the student during initial discussions. By reframing the question and determining the student's beliefs and motivations, the counselor can assign the appropriate strategic tasks. This process is important to the success of the counseling.

43. C: ASCA's Annual Calendar template is used to report the schedule for all classroom and group activities. The Classroom and Group Mindsets and Behaviors Action Plan presents the topics addressed for each lesson on the annual calendar. The Annual Student Outcome Goal Plan is a one-page report used to identify outcome data and goals targeting a subset of students. The Closing-the-Gap Action Plan/Results Report includes goals, measurement methods, and outcome measures used to determine discrepancies in learning or outcomes.

44. C: This training method is intended to increase consulting and interviewing skills for the counselor. This model comprises seven steps:

1. *Establishing a consulting relationship* involves relationship building and goal setting with the client.
2. *Identifying and clarifying the problem situation* requires a counselor to hear beyond what is being said in order to uncover any underlying problems.
3. *Determining the desired outcome* is a simple restatement of the problem and goals.

4. *Developing ideas and strategies* requires the client and counselor to set objectives for achieving the goals.
5. *Developing a plan* requires the counselor and client to determine the best course of action for implementing objectives and achieving goals.
6. *Specifying the plan* serves to further determine the specific steps for success.
7. *Confirming the consulting relationship* will be complete when the student understands the problem-solving process and is comfortable with the plan of action developed with the counselor.

45. B: Solution-focused brief counseling always focuses on the exception to the problem, improvements since the previous session, and progress toward the goal. Therefore, most subsequent sessions will begin with the counselor asking the client about what has improved since the previous session.

46. C: Standardized achievement tests measure an individual's skill or knowledge in a specific subject area. In this case, the test was designed to measure the student's mastery of grade-level skills and concepts in math. The student's score of "not proficient" indicates that the student did not demonstrate mastery of all of these skills. This may be a result of the instruction the student received. However, it should not be interpreted as a demonstration of low, or comparatively lower, intelligence.

47. B: There are a number of factors that can affect students, especially during middle and high school. In this case, it would be wise to initially discuss problems with peers with this student. Social problems are often a cause of problems in school, including a marked drop in grades. If this student is having problems with a boyfriend, it may be important to determine the seriousness of the problems, as abusive relationships in schools do occur. Since this student typically does well in school, the difficulty level of the classes would not be the major concern, unless she recently began new advanced courses. While there is nothing given about a history indicating that she may have problems with self-esteem or mental health issues, it is best to start with the most straightforward and common causes.

48. D: Skill practice is typically not a stated goal of a support group and would not be appropriate in this situation. Skill practice would be more appropriate for an educational or therapy group.

49. C: Counselors deliver direct (i.e., face-to-face) services to students through appraisal, advisement, counseling, and instruction. Appraisal involves administering inventories, surveys, and tests to assess a student's achievement, skills, and interests. Advisement is the process of reviewing appraisal data and making recommendations. Consultation, referral, and collaboration are indirect services used to promote each student's equitable access to services and advance systemic change.

50. A: Contracts or pledges to refrain from drug/alcohol use are generally not very effective, just like with suicide contracts. ASCA and the National Institute on Drug Abuse discuss the evidence-based best practices for drug abuse prevention. Factual education about the risks and effects of drug/alcohol use, especially the effects of drug/alcohol use on the adolescent brain, is an effective component of a comprehensive program. A stress management component is important because many students view drug/alcohol use as a means to reduce or cope with stress. Many evidence-based programs include components and education designed to reduce risk factors (such as aggressive behavior and poverty) and boost protective factors (such as self-control and academic competence). While schools do not always have control over the risk factors students may have, a comprehensive program can strengthen the protective factors, which can mitigate the effects of those risk factors.

51. B: Outcome data is the data that measures the positive impact of the intervention. In the case of a small group focused on improving attendance, students' attendance rates at the conclusion of the small group represent a measurable impact. Meeting logs tracking student attendance at the small group meetings would be an example of process data, while post-tests and self-evaluations would both be examples of perception data.

52. D: Participation data indicates the number of students participating in a comprehensive school counseling program, the activities provided, and the length of time allotted for the activities. Outcome data captures how the activity affects attendance, achievement, and discipline measures. Disaggregating data is the process of separating data sets to determine trends and patterns. Mindsets and Behaviors data encompasses the knowledge, attitudes, and skills necessary for social/emotional, career, and academic achievement.

53. B: The Holland Code Assessment, or RIASEC Test, provides a three-letter interest code resulting from a combination of the following six personality types and work environments: Realistic (R), Investigative (I), Artistic (A), Social (S), Enterprising (E), and Conventional (C). The National Career Clusters Framework is a career technical education (CTE) program that uses 16 career clusters to provide nearly 80 career pathways. The Employability Skills Framework emphasizes attaining soft skills like those contained in ASCA's Mindsets and Behaviors student standards. The Myers-Briggs Type Inventory results include 16 personality types resulting from the four preferences: Introversion/Extraversion, Sensing/Intuition, Thinking/Feeling, and Judging/Perceiving.

54. B: A needs assessment is a type of perception data that is commonly used to plan a comprehensive school counseling program. Needs assessments help a counselor identify areas of strength and need in their school in order to make decisions about programming. Although the school data profile is another helpful document outlining data that can be used to plan a school counseling program, it is not a type of perception data. The school data profile focuses on demographic and outcome data. Pre-test data is a type of perception data, but it wouldn't be used to plan a comprehensive school counseling program; instead, pre-test data could be used to evaluate prior knowledge of a topic or to compare to the post-test data to establish the effectiveness of an intervention. Finally, achievement testing data is a type of outcome data, and while it can be part of the planning process (for example, it is part of the school data profile), achievement testing data alone would not provide enough information to plan a comprehensive school counseling program.

55. A: The elementary counselor is focused on foundational social/emotional skills and academic mindsets, as well as intervention and prevention. By middle school, counselors increase the focus on positive social skills and helping students achieve their academic potential while setting future career goals. High school counselors have the strongest focus on helping students achieving academic potential and setting career goals, with additional focuses on social skills and personal growth.

56. A: The Wechsler Intelligence Scale for Children (WISC) is a commonly used tool in a psycho-educational evaluation, typically as part of a special education evaluation; however, it is inappropriate to use an intelligence test as the sole basis for special education placement decisions. For example, if a student has a suspected learning disability, an average or above-average IQ score should not be used to deny them special education services. It is also inappropriate to use IQ test results to choose students' coursework, career guidance, or college options. Assessments represent only one data point in making decisions about a student's education.

57. A: Bloom's taxonomy of educational objectives describes six levels of knowledge. At the lowest level, Knowledge is the ability to name and identify things. Comprehension occurs when a student can explain a topic or concept. Application refers to a student's ability to use information in the real world. Analysis is the ability to analyze and make comparisons. Synthesis is the ability to develop hypotheses and produce results. Finally, the highest level in Bloom's taxonomy is Evaluation, which refers to the ability to assess and critique an idea or concept. Assessments should touch on all six levels of learning. By making sure all levels in Bloom's taxonomy are covered, the counselor will have an indication of areas that need improvement and what level of understanding to focus on. For example, a student may be able to identify parts of a sentence but not understand how to analyze that sentence. The intervention would then focus more on sentence analysis and less on defining parts of the sentence.

58. B: The zone of proximal development describes the concepts or skills beyond what a learner is able to do on their own, or the "zone" where the learner can accomplish a new task or skill with the help of someone else. This is a key component of Vygotsky's social development theory.

59. B: The Strong Interest Inventory is a career assessment designed to help individuals understand their interests and how they relate to different types of careers. The Strong Interest Inventory is based on the work of John Holland and the concept that people with similar interests work in similar careers.

60. D: Each of the first three answer choices describes a topic or task that would be addressed in the group selection process. Informed consent, parent permission, and voluntary participation would all be established in the individual interview and invitation to the group. Allaying anxiety is typically addressed in the initial group meeting or "forming" stage of the group.

61. C: A counselor must always take into consideration the cultural barriers and needs of students and their families. In situations where language barriers are present, a counselor should offer a translator during any meeting. This will ensure that the parents receive the correct information. This will also show the parents that they are welcome and accepted into the school. When they are offered translation services, parents may become more comfortable, which means that their participation with the school and their children's education will increase. Another effective strategy is to offer free or low-cost English courses. While a counselor cannot require anyone to take these courses, making them available to those who are interested will be beneficial to families.

62. B: School counselors are ethically obligated to provide a list of multiple district-vetted individuals rather than matching students with one individual. Section A.6.b. of the 2022 ASCA Ethical Standards for School Counselors states that school counselors are "careful not to indicate an endorsement or preference for one individual or practice." Additional considerations include ensuring that the referral does not serve the counselor's personal interests, that a collaborative relationship with outside providers is established, and that a release of information is signed to protect confidentiality.

63. C: Continued education for parents is not typically considered a type of parent involvement. Involvement begins at the parenting level. Schools cannot tell individuals how to parent; however, they can provide information for parents about encouraging good academic practices while at home. For example, informing parents about the appropriate amount of time their child should spend on homework is one strategy. Communication is the next level of participation. Sending home progress reports and holding conferences both increase communication between schools and parents. The third level involves volunteering, which can include one-time projects or long-term participation. The last three levels involve learning at home. Examples of this are providing information on the skills their children will learn throughout the school year, decision-making by encouraging participating on a school advisory board, and collaboration with the community.

64. C: The School Counselor Performance Appraisal is a part of the Accountability component of an ASCA National Model program. The specifics of the tools used to complete the appraisal are based on school, district, or state guidelines and processes. ASCA recommends that School Counselor Performance Appraisals include a self-evaluation component in addition to an administrative evaluation and assessment of goal attainment. Like all program evaluation tools, the School Counselor Performance Appraisal should be based on a variety of data. This tool can be utilized by the school counselor and school administrators to make program decisions and adjustments.

65. B: Developmental career theories focus on career development throughout a lifespan. While earlier theories such as the trait-factor approach focus on a single decision of the "best" job for life, developmental theories identify various stages an individual goes through in the process of their career development. Ginzberg and associates identified three stages (fantasy, tentative, and realistic), while Super identified five (growth, exploration, establishment, maintenance, and decline). Contemporary developmental career theories do not generally view an early-adulthood cut-off to the career development process.

66. C: Assisting students with course selections to help students make choices that are rigorous and align with their post-secondary plans is an appropriate activity for a school counselor. Understanding appropriate and inappropriate counseling tasks is a major focus of the Management section of the ASCA National Model; this is an area that school counselors should be very familiar with in order to plan their use of time and advocate for appropriate duties. A comprehensive school counseling program designed with the ASCA National Model will focus on prevention, intervention, and advocacy, not clerical or administrative tasks. When it comes to assisting students with post-secondary plans, there are many tasks that school counselors may have done historically or may still do in some schools that are not considered appropriate activities. These include tasks such as calculating class rank or grade point average, coordinating schoolwide SAT testing, copying student records for college applications, or doing other clerical tasks related to college applications.

67. C: When taking an assessment relating to topics that may be socially undesirable, individuals have a tendency to report answers that conform to mainstream society. In this case, students may be afraid of getting in trouble if they answer positively in response to questions about drug or alcohol use. Conversely, if this assessment is given in a group setting, students may want to "show off" to their peers by giving a greater number of positive answers. While this type of assessment may provide the counselor with preliminary results, the results may be skewed. This type of assessment should always include a variety of questions in different forms in order to validate findings and to control for false answers.

68. B: This type of scaling can be beneficial for a preliminary view of a student's thoughts on a topic. However, providing only four choices means that the student must choose in a positive or negative direction. This can produce skewed results and lead the counselor to believe that a majority of students are for or against a topic, when in fact students may be neutral on some topics but are required to make a decision. For example, consider the following statement: "Morning announcements are a waste of time." This statement may elicit a neutral response for students; however, without a neutral option to select, they are forced to agree or disagree. If students choose a negative answer, does this necessarily indicate that they would like more announcements in the morning? Conversely, if students respond positively, does this indicate that they want no morning announcements?

69. B: Although using this type of assessment may result in more neutral responses, most individuals will provide their true thoughts. Receiving an assessment with all neutral responses should be considered an outlier. Depending on the purpose of the assessment, the counselor may consider disregarding it in the results and providing an explanation in any required report. Depending on the nature of the assessment, the counselor can conduct additional assessments with the student to determine any difficulties this student may be having. Regardless, when giving students surveys, it must be indicated that all responses are confidential, and the students should respond as honestly as possible.

70. D: Teachers, along with other helping professionals such as counselors, nurses, and physical therapists, closely align with the social personality type. Examples of the other personality types include: realistic (pilot, surveyor), investigative (astronomer, physician), artistic (writer, designer), enterprising (lawyer, salesperson), and conventional (accountant, actuary).

71. D: According to the ASCA Mindsets and Behaviors for Student Success, there are two major categories of standards relating to student development, which can be applied to all three domains of a comprehensive counseling program (academic, social/emotional, college/career). The two major categories are Mindset Standards and Behavior Standards, and Behavior Standards are further broken down into learning strategies, self-management skills, and social skills subcategories. Each of these categories of standards would be a major component of a comprehensive guidance program. Emotional regulation skills would more likely be addressed in individual or small group counseling (such as a small group focused on anger management or an individual counseling session focused on calming strategies).

72. B: The gatekeeper of a group is the member who tries to keep everyone else on task and ensure they are participating in the group. The scapegoat is the group member whom everyone else tries to blame when things go wrong. The energizer is the group member who attempts to get others excited and enthusiastic about the group, and the interrogator asks a lot of questions of the group.

73. C: ASCA's information-gathering tool for suicide concerns emphasizes directly engaging with students rather than leaving them alone with self-assessment instruments. ASCA endorses the Suicide Information Conversation Guide, which underscores the importance of a guided conversation with minimum standards that include directly asking the student about suicide and access to means and engaging both the student and supportive individuals in safety planning.

74. D: Counselors must respect the cultural identity of their students. Since the student is not seeing the counselor because of cultural identity issues, it would be considered professionally inappropriate for the counselor to focus on her Chinese heritage unprompted. It is, however, the counselor's responsibility to understand this student's cultural identity in order to develop effective interventions for this student's presenting problem. The counselor must also have a clear understanding of her own beliefs and stereotypes in this situation that may cause bias when treating this student. Counselors who are unaware of these issues may inadvertently treat a student of another culture with negativity or less support than she would a student of her own culture.

75. B: When it comes to providing equal access to the curriculum via a Section 504 plan or IEP, the most common terms used are "accommodation" and "modification." While counselors will frequently hear and use these terms in conjunction with each other, they refer to different types of strategies. Accommodations are those strategies that change the environment, time, type of output, or size of the task at hand without fundamentally changing the task, instructional level, or content that the student is learning. Accommodations allow students to access the curriculum as well as their non-disabled peers and perform the same learning tasks as their peers. Preferential seating (such as seating away from distractions or close to the teacher) is an example of environmental accommodation. Extended time is an accommodation that changes the length of time given to complete a task without changing the task itself. Modifications, however, change the task or content itself based on a child's needs. Modifications may lower or change the learning standards expected of the student. An example of a modification would be giving a child an alternative reading passage on their reading level. Interventions are instructional strategies used to help a child learn content; an example would be small group instruction.

76. D: Counselors frequently make referrals to connect their students with appropriate resources to support their needs. Counselors may make internal referrals, which include referrals to school staff such as the nurse, principal, psychologist, intervention team, and so forth. Answer choices A, B, and C all give examples of internal referrals. Choices A and B are examples of appropriate referrals, while choice C is not appropriate for the student's needs. Students expressing suicidal ideation should be evaluated by a mental health professional and referred in accordance with school and district policies; school psychologists are typically not qualified mental health providers. External referrals could be made to community resources, social services, mental health organizations, or any other person or service that takes place outside of the school environment.

77. B: Standardized tests pose many problems for students who are learning English as a second language. Not only do students face the difficulty of taking an assessment in a language other than their native language, but often these students struggle with cultural references within the assessments as well. For example, if a test includes a reading passage about an American holiday like the Fourth of July, students who are immigrants may not understand the references being made due to their unfamiliarity with that particular cultural experience. Therefore, even if tests are translated into a student's native language, it is still possible that the test will be invalid due to cultural references or even translation errors. Due to the vast number of languages and dialects spoken by students, it is unlikely that an assessment has been translated and validated in every language spoken by students in schools.

78. C: School counselors should never be the sole decision-makers in any part of the IEP process; instead, they should serve as members of a multi-disciplinary team working together to meet the needs of students with special needs. According to ASCA, school counselors provide only short-term, goal-focused counseling as an IEP-related service; long-term or therapeutic counseling should be provided by other qualified mental health professionals (e.g., school psychologists, social workers, or community providers) rather than being written into an IEP as a school counselor service. Writing and determining the specific social-emotional goals in the IEP is the responsibility of the entire IEP team and typically the special education case manager; the school counselor contributes data and suggestions but does not unilaterally write IEP goals. Therefore, (C) is not an accurate description of the counselor's role, whereas (A), (B), and (D) are.

79. B: Discussion groups are effective ways to get parents and students involved in learning about cultural diversity. These discussion groups can offer participants the opportunity to talk about their particular cultures. Additionally, these groups offer a nonthreatening venue for others to ask questions and work out misunderstandings about various cultures that have been perpetuated by stereotypes. These groups also offer parents and students the chance to celebrate different cultures through activities. In addition to group discussions about participants' cultures, discussions about various types of families and lifestyles are beneficial. For example, biracial families, families with adopted or foster children, and families with stepparents are increasingly common in American society, and education about these various types of families is just as important as learning about other cultures.

80. C: Calculating grade point averages is an inappropriate activity for school counselors, according to the ASCA National Model. Providing core classroom guidance curriculum is an appropriate direct service, as is counseling students about appropriate dress for school. While counselors should not be responsible for maintaining student records, it is appropriate for counselors to ensure regulations are followed in the maintenance of those records.

Practice Test #2

1. A counselor is working individually with a student toward their goal of developing friendships and feeling more connected at school. According to the theory of solution-focused brief therapy, how would the counselor approach termination of the student's individual counseling sessions?

a. Wait until the student reports that they are at a 10/10 on the scaling question.
b. Terminate after six sessions, as anything longer is not "brief."
c. Ask the student how they will know when they no longer need individual counseling.
d. Wait until the counselor observes that the student has achieved their goal.

2. Counselors are often responsible for initiating a parent conference by making a phone call or sending a letter home. What should a counselor do in order to avoid an automatic negative reaction from parents?

a. State all the problems their child is having.
b. Speak with a level of equality and openness.
c. State that things at home must change.
d. Suggest that their child seek additional help.

3. A seven-year-old student is engaged in a classroom guidance session focused on friendship skills. The student comments that "It is important to take turns, otherwise you will get in trouble with the teacher." This student's comment best aligns with which stage of moral development, according to Lawrence Kohlberg?

a. Obedience and punishment (stage 1)
b. Maintaining personal relationships (stage 3)
c. Law and order (stage 4)
d. Social contract (stage 5)

4. Which of the following is not a section within the Assess component of the ASCA National Model?

a. Program
b. School Counselor
c. Annual Results Reports
d. Student impact

5. A school counselor plans to advocate with their school district for an appropriate counselor-to-student ratio. Which of the following would be the most appropriate and effective data source to support their request?

a. Counselor use-of-time assessment
b. ASCA research publications
c. Counseling program annual calendar
d. Recognized ASCA Model Program

6. Mr. Smith, a school counselor, is serving on an IEP team for a student with severe social-emotional needs. The IEP team brings up the need for the student to have individual counseling focused on these needs. Which of the following statements would be an appropriate response from Mr. Smith in this situation?

a. It is inappropriate for a school counselor to provide individual counseling to a student as part of their IEP, as they are not certified special education staff.
b. It is appropriate for a school counselor to provide individual counseling to a student as part of their IEP, but no more than once per week.
c. It is inappropriate for a school counselor to provide individual counseling to a student as part of their IEP, as it is not an approved special education service.
d. It is appropriate for a school counselor to provide individual counseling to a student as part of their IEP, but only on a short-term basis for a specific goal.

Refer to the following for question 7:

Mrs. Johnson is a middle school counselor who has been working with a seventh-grade student in individual counseling. The student was diagnosed by an outside therapist with an anxiety disorder and regularly earns failing grades on tests despite excellent classwork and homework grades. Mrs. Johnson convenes a team meeting to discuss appropriate accommodations for the student under Section 504. Since she has other students that also struggle with anxiety disorders, she is also considering adding the student to a small counseling group.

7. Which role of the school counselor was Mrs. Johnson primarily demonstrating in this situation?

a. Advocate
b. Collaborator
c. Leader
d. Consultant

8. A school utilizes a reward system in which students can exchange tickets for small prizes. A student at the school has been demonstrating the behavior of blurting out answers instead of raising his hand. When he raises his hand before blurting out an answer, his teacher gives him a ticket for a prize. According to B.F. Skinner's operant conditioning theory, the ticket represents which type of consequence?

a. Positive reinforcement
b. Negative reinforcement
c. Punishment
d. Neutral consequence

Refer to the following for question 9:

A school counselor leading a counseling group for students whose parents are going through a separation or divorce generally sits and listens to the group's conversations but does not participate in the conversations or provide direction to the group.

9. Which group leadership style is this counselor demonstrating?

a. Autocratic
b. Democratic
c. Laissez-faire
d. Authoritarian

10. According to ASCA, which of the following is an appropriate use of standardized testing results?

a. Using standardized test scores to determine students' eligibility to enroll in advanced coursework
b. Disaggregating standardized test scores to guide programming and instructional decisions
c. Basing promotion and retention decisions on standardized test scores
d. Determining a student's eligibility for Section 504 services based on their standardized test scores

11. Which of the following is an example of consultation?

a. Two school counselors work together to plan a schoolwide classroom guidance curriculum.
b. A school counselor and principal meet to sign an annual agreement before the school year starts.
c. A school counselor meets with the school's speech therapist to learn about strategies to support a student who stutters.
d. A school counselor participates in an IEP team meeting to determine appropriate services for a student with a learning disability.

12. A school counselor uses the School Data Summary Template in conjunction with the school's Student Information System to determine school counseling priorities. Engaging in this annual process allows the counselor to:

a. Efficiently monitor and measure ASCA SMART goals
b. Track Excel chart disaggregated data over time
c. Organize individualized student improvement plans
d. Track trends among student subgroups

13. Ms. Joseph, a school counselor, has been working with an anxious student individually for several weeks. It is clear that the child's needs are significant and the anxiety is interfering with his ability to attend school. Ms. Joseph recognizes that her training is not adequate for the needs of the student. What is Ms. Joseph's ethical obligation in this scenario?

a. Ms. Joseph should seek additional training and development in this area in order to better support the student.
b. Ms. Joseph should refer the child's parents to a counselor she knows who has been effective with other anxious students in the past.
c. Ms. Joseph should stop seeing the child and tell his parents that he should see an outside counselor.
d. Ms. Joseph should provide the child's parents with a list of referrals and continue working with the child in the meantime.

14. Which of the following scenarios is in violation of the Family Educational Rights and Privacy Act (FERPA)?

a. A 16-year-old student asks to view their educational record and is permitted to do so without parental consent.
b. A non-custodial parent asks to inspect their child's educational record and is permitted to do so without the custodial parent's consent.
c. A parent asks to review their child's educational record and then requests an item that they believe to be inaccurate be removed from the record.
d. A school creates a directory of student contact information and allows parents a 30-day notice to opt out of the directory.

15. Which of the following is NOT an appropriate use of end-of-grade standardized test scores?

a. Identifying an individual student's academic strengths
b. Improving classroom instructional plans
c. Determining eligibility for special education services
d. Tracking an individual student's academic growth

16. The school counselor's first step in completing the ASCA Fourth Edition Annual Administrative Conference Template is to provide findings from which of the following?

a. The Classroom and Small Group Results Report
b. The School Data Summary
c. The Classroom Mindsets and Behaviors Action Plan
d. The Annual Student Outcome Goals

17. For students who disobey the rules on fighting, rather than requiring them to serve a silent detention, you suggest conducting a problem-centered, structured intervention group. What issues should you focus on during this group?

a. Self-actualization
b. Aggressive behaviors
c. Safety
d. Physiological issues

18. Mr. Preston is conducting a conflict resolution session between two 3rd-grade boys after an altercation at recess. Sam is upset because he wanted to play soccer with a group of boys, and Kyle told him he couldn't play. Kyle was the team captain, so the other boys went along with what he said, and Sam wasn't able to join the game. Sam feels left out and sad; Kyle says that he likes playing with Sam, but Sam is not a good soccer player and would have made his team lose. Which of the following possible resolutions represents a collaborative outcome?

a. Sam agrees to do something else at recess so that Kyle's team won't lose the game.
b. Kyle agrees to play a different game at recess so that Sam won't feel left out.
c. Kyle agrees to only play soccer every other day, alternating with a different game that Sam can play.
d. Kyle and Sam agree to practice soccer skills together so that Sam improves and they can play together.

19. Professional counselors are expected to contribute to the profession of counseling. What is one way for counselors to participate and contribute?

a. Maintain an active case load.
b. Hold group sessions for students.
c. Participate in professional associations.
d. Maintain their licensure regardless of whether they are currently providing counseling services.

20. When administering a standardized test, such as an end-of-grade test, certain conditions must be maintained in order for the test results to be valid. Which of the following conditions would NOT impact the validity of a standardized end-of-grade reading test?

a. Altering the length of time provided for the test
b. Changing the number of items on the test
c. Explaining a test question in simpler terms
d. Administering the test at a different time of day

21. Mrs. Mason is a high school counselor who has been working with a 9th-grade student in individual counseling for a month. During their first three sessions together, it becomes clear that the student has significant depression and has not experienced any improvement during the course of individual counseling thus far. Which of the following is the most appropriate next step for Mrs. Mason?

a. Sign up for a webinar about depression to learn new strategies to help the student.
b. Call a local mental health facility for a crisis evaluation on the student.
c. Seek professional advice from another school counselor in the district.
d. Work with the student and their parent to refer the child to an outside mental health provider.

22. Parents can be involved in the school in a number of ways. You would like to increase parent participation in the career resource room at the school. In addition to contacting the PTA, how else might a counselor recruit parents to volunteer?

a. Distribute annual surveys for parents to identify their volunteer interests and abilities.
b. The PTA is the only place to find volunteers.
c. Place an ad in the newspaper.
d. Recruit teachers because they are easier to contact.

23. Which of the following resources would best be used to help a school counselor complete the use-of-time assessment?

a. The school district's student information system
b. Data collected from an online survey
c. A digital calendar, such as Google Calendar
d. Documentation of the counselor's sick leave

24. Which of the following describes a method a school counselor could utilize to collect perception data in order to measure the effectiveness of a closing-the-gap action plan?

a. Comparing schoolwide academic data from before and after the intervention
b. Comparing pre- and post-tests of the student competencies targeted during the intervention
c. Completing sign-in sheets to track attendance at each portion of the intervention
d. Collecting schoolwide student surveys from before and after the intervention

25. An elementary school principal asks the school counselor to teach a health course and give students grades. What is the counselor's ethical obligation?

a. To agree to teach the course if another staff member covers the counselor's duties during instructional time
b. To tell the principal that teaching the course may place students at risk and that assigning grades leads to a dual relationship
c. To agree to teach the course if it aligns with the ASCA Student Standards Mindsets and Behaviors for Student Success but decline to assign grades
d. To request that the course be incorporated into the comprehensive school counseling plan and seek consultation to ensure ethical guidelines are followed

26. A middle school counselor is planning an anti-bullying curriculum for classroom guidance lessons. Which of the following statements is NOT true about middle school students and bullying?

a. Middle school girls are more likely to experience social bullying than physical bullying.
b. Middle school students are likely to experience or participate in cyberbullying.
c. Middle school students who are "bystanders" are encouraging bullying to continue.
d. Middle school boys and girls experience and participate in social bullying to equal degrees.

27. When a diagnostic assessment for learning needs is conducted, what factor is NOT considered?

a. Prior knowledge
b. Interests
c. Learning style preferences
d. Sociability

28. The ASCA Mindsets & Behaviors for Student Success outlines standards or student learning that can be addressed through a classroom guidance curriculum. Which of the four components of the ASCA National Model Program includes these standards?

a. Define
b. Manage
c. Deliver
d. Assess

29. For comprehensive school counseling programs to be effective and efficient, they must be integrated into the total educational process. This is BEST accomplished by school counselors:

a. Serving on leadership teams
b. Sharing in administrative duties
c. Delivering programs that improve shared outcomes
d. Collaborating with staff on school-wide initiatives

30. Which of the following is NOT a type of results report completed as part of a school counseling program evaluation?

a. Curriculum results report
b. Individual results report
c. Small-group results report
d. Closing-the-gap results report

31. In reviewing student outcome data, a school counselor notes that the overall attendance rate of 7th-grade students is much lower than that of 6th- or 8th-grade students. Which of the following is a possible intervention the school counselor could implement based on this piece of data?

a. Surveying 7th-grade students to learn about their feelings about school
b. Initiating a small group focused on improving school attendance
c. Planning classroom guidance for 7th graders focused on improving school attendance
d. Organizing an advisory council to solicit stakeholder feedback on school attendance

Refer to the following for question 32:

At the beginning of a counseling relationship, the counselor informs the student of confidentiality, stating that he cannot reveal anything that is discussed during the sessions no matter what. After a few sessions, the counselor feels that the student would benefit from extra sessions and offers to meet the student outside of school to talk over coffee. During these after-school sessions, the student informs the counselor that she is considering suicide. Since the counselor does not think this student will follow through, he disregards the statement.

32. What exception relating to confidentiality did the counselor neglect to discuss with the student?

a. Pregnancy
b. Harm to self or others
c. Sexual relationships
d. Problems with self-esteem

33. A high school counselor spends 20 minutes on the phone with a student's mental health therapist, discussing how school personnel can help to ensure the safety of the student after a recent mental health crisis. This is an example of which type of task?

a. Individual student planning
b. Responsive services
c. Consultation
d. Creating an action plan

34. A school counselor meets with parents concerned about their child's reading score results on a normed achievement test. The counselor sees that the student's stanine score on the reading subtest is 6. What does this indicate?

a. The student's raw score in reading is 6.
b. The student's score is one standard deviation below the mean.
c. The student received a 6th-grade-equivalent score.
d. The student scored in the 60th to 76th percentile.

35. A school counselor working to create an academic intervention plan for a student is most likely to utilize which of the following approaches to develop the plan?

a. Strengths-based focus
b. Problem identification
c. Cognitive behavioral therapy
d. Family therapy

36. What is the main premise behind a developmental guidance program?

a. All students develop at different rates, so various programs must be designed.
b. Guidance programs are developmental in nature, beginning with simple concepts and progressing to more abstract concepts.
c. Developmental guidance programs are used for students with developmental disabilities to help them achieve their full potential.
d. Developmental guidance programs focus on human development and positive self-concepts.

37. What is the primary purpose of assessing a comprehensive school counseling program (CSCP)?

a. To define the standards and competencies of professional practice
b. To determine direct and indirect methods for delivering the program
c. To analyze progress toward successful implementation of the program
d. To guide the planning, organizing, and implementation of the program

38. As a high school counselor, you observe that the number of pregnant teens on campus has been increasing over the past few years. What steps can you put into place to address this issue?

a. Continue to focus on student academics.
b. Allow pregnant students to have a lighter course load in order to focus on their health and the pregnancy.
c. Develop prevention and intervention programs to address this issue.
d. Counsel students on the difficulties of having a child at this age and assist with federal aid paperwork.

39. Which of the following school counselor roles is considered a direct service?

a. Consulting
b. Collaborating
c. Evaluating
d. Counseling

40. Young girls who experience abuse in the home or in a relationship have increased risk factors including:

a. Drug abuse
b. Teen pregnancy
c. Poor grades
d. All of the above

41. Which of the following would be considered an educational group?

a. A group focused on processing grief and loss.
b. A group focused on teaching parenting skills.
c. A group focused on planning a school event.
d. A group focused on overcoming test anxiety.

42. One of the essential roles of a school counselor is consultation. Consultation is considered which type of service?

a. Responsive service
b. Individual student planning
c. School counseling core curriculum
d. Indirect student service

43. There is little parent involvement in many schools due to large numbers of working parents. What is one strategy to use to increase participation?

a. Offer incentives for participation.
b. Focus on the unemployed parents to work with.
c. Suggest holding meetings and events on the weekends.
d. Offer opportunities at various times during the week.

44. When beginning a program evaluation, what documentation will be necessary?

a. Satisfaction surveys from previous program sessions
b. A list of programs offered
c. The number of participants in last year's programs
d. Guidance curriculum guides

45. James is a middle school student in a counseling group. During a group session, the school counselor notices that James has been more withdrawn and has not been participating in the group discussion. Which of the following strategies would be an appropriate response to this observation?

a. Ignore James's non-participation, as group participation is voluntary.
b. Pull James aside during the group session and have a conversation with him about his participation.
c. Make a connection between James and another group member.
d. Remove James from the group, as his non-participation is threatening other group members' progress.

46. How might training workshops be misperceived by parents?

a. Parents are uneducated.
b. Parents do not welcome additional training.
c. They see such programs as trying to change their core values and methods of raising their children.
d. They have problem children.

47. Hanna is a new kindergarten student who is legally blind. Her parents talk to the school counselor during the enrollment process and ask for information about the services and supports their daughter will be able to access in school. Which of the following laws or programs would the counselor refer to in order to provide guidance about Hanna's situation?

a. IDEA
b. Section 504
c. FERPA
d. ESSA

48. Compared to middle school or high school counselors, elementary school counselors must have an especially strong understanding of what?

a. Child development
b. Continued education options
c. Relationship building
d. Adjustment and coping mechanisms

49. A supervisor for a counseling program collects outcomes data for all clients who received services last year. When plotting the distribution, the supervisor notices that clients younger than age 12 have measures skewed to the left. Which of the following is true of distributions skewed to the left (i.e., negatively skewed)?

a. The mean is less than the median.
b. The mean is greater than the median.
c. The mean and the median are the same value.
d. The mode is the lowest value.

50. A school counselor is conducting student training for a peer mediation program. She is writing role-play scripts for students to act out various types of communication strategies they may use in the peer mediation process. Which of the following script phrases represents a communication approach or technique that she would NOT want her students to practice using in the peer mediation process?

a. "I think you should..."
b. "Can you tell me more?"
c. "What I hear you saying is..."
d. "I can see why you feel that way."

51. A school counselor wishes to perform a formal assessment of their comprehensive school counseling program but is receiving some pushback from stakeholders. Which of the following is the best rationale for a program assessment?

a. To meet mandatory school district requirements
b. To determine if any improvements need to be made
c. To show how a subset of students has been impacted
d. To guide interventions for Tier 2 and Tier 3 students

52. Which of the following is NOT true about mentor-mentee programs for students?

a. Mentor-mentee programs have a positive impact on student academic achievement.
b. Mentor-mentee programs are a tier I intervention for students at risk.
c. Mentor-mentee programs require parent permission for students to participate.
d. Mentor-mentee programs have a positive impact on the number of disciplinary referrals.

53. Which of the following school counselor activities does NOT take place within the Manage component of the ASCA National Model?

a. Completing a use-of-time assessment
b. Analyzing a results report
c. Creating a closing-the-gap action plan
d. Writing a mission and vision statement

54. A school counselor conducts a needs assessment with students and staff. Using the data gathered from the needs assessment, the counselor could do all of the following EXCEPT:

a. Identify small-group counseling topics
b. Design classroom guidance curriculum
c. Identify individual student needs
d. Evaluate the previous year's program

55. On which of the components of a comprehensive school counseling program should a counselor ideally spend the majority of their time?

a. Define
b. Manage
c. Deliver
d. Assess

56. Which of the following is an example of consultation services?

a. Advising a colleague on reporting suspected cases of child abuse
b. Helping a teacher develop grade-appropriate classroom rules
c. Serving as district representative on career development committees
d. Providing ongoing teacher training on how to recognize mental health warning signs

57. A counselor is leading an assertiveness training group based on cognitive behavioral therapy. Which of the following techniques would most likely be used in this specific type of group?

a. Role-playing
b. Linking and encouraging
c. Unstructured techniques
d. Empty chair

58. Solution-focused brief counseling consists of what six steps?

a. Define problem, determine goals, develop intervention, assign strategic tasks, emphasize positive behavior, terminate counseling
b. Define problem, determine goals, develop intervention, revisit goals, develop a second intervention, terminate counseling
c. Conduct psychoanalysis, determine underlying problem, develop group intervention plan, reinforce behavior, assign strategic task, terminate counseling
d. Identify prevention steps, define problem, determine goals, develop intervention, assign strategic task, terminate counseling

59. Mr. Dean, a school counseling student in a graduate program, is applying for internship positions for the upcoming school year and is required to carry professional liability insurance. What is the best method for Mr. Dean to acquire a complete professional liability policy?

a. Contact his university field experiences office
b. Contact the local school district to be added to their district policy
c. Join the National Board for Certified Counselors
d. Join ASCA as a student member

60. A counselor has developed a comprehensive developmental counseling program in a large school. This program consists of daily meetings and programs to address the various needs of students. In order to avoid burnout, how might the counselor effectively manage so many meetings and programs?

a. Schedule meetings a few hours after school ends so she or he can take a break.
b. Recruit the help of teachers and peer mentors to assist with the programs.
c. Try to combine groups so that there are not so many.
d. Rely on consultants to run the programs that are scheduled for after school.

Refer to the following for question 61:

A 5-year-old boy continues to attempt to play with children who openly ridicule him and leave him out of games. His persistence with this group of children has recently resulted in a number of fights on the playground. After being referred to your office, you learn that he has an unsupportive home life. His parents were divorced last year. He lives with his mother, who works at night, and he does not see his father. He is often left at home alone; however, a neighbor watches him from time to time.

61. According to Pavlov's theory of development, what would you expect to occur in terms of this child's learning and behavior?

a. Nothing; he would naturally continue to try to fit in.
b. The child would become conditioned to the negative response and avoid the situation.
c. The child would take cues from his social environment and act accordingly.
d. The child would grow out of this stage and soon make friends.

62. A school counselor is meeting with the parent of a student in order to discuss the parent's concerns about their child's academic progress. The parent is unsure of how to interpret their child's standardized test results from the state's end-of-grade, norm-referenced tests. Which of the following explanations of the child's test results is accurate for this type of test?

a. "Your child's percentile score compares their performance to their same-age peers across the state."
b. "Your child's percentile score indicates the number of test questions they answered correctly."
c. "Your child's percentile score indicates the percentage of grade-level standards they mastered this year."
d. "Your child's percentile score indicates their potential for success in the next grade level."

63. How can a school counselor best serve students identified as having serious emotional disturbances?

a. Supervise individualized education program (IEP) implementation.
b. Engage in community advocacy for individuals with emotional disabilities.
c. Provide long-term counseling and supportive services.
d. Provide written addendums to 504 plans and IEPs when necessary.

64. Jim, a member of a counseling group focused on overcoming social anxiety, shares his recent success with utilizing skills learned from the group to navigate a tricky social situation. Jim is excited about his success and how the skills he learned helped him in that situation; the other members of the group are excited for him as well. Which benefit of group counseling would be directly demonstrated by this scenario?

a. Installation of hope
b. Universality
c. Group cohesiveness
d. Imparting information

65. Which of the following student differences would NOT be a likely cause of cultural bias on a test?

a. Differences in English proficiency
b. Differences in socioeconomic status
c. Differences in classroom grouping
d. Differences in gender

66. Which of the following ASCA National Model documents is used to identify and communicate school counseling program priorities to all stakeholders?

a. Annual calendar
b. Annual agreement
c. School data profile
d. Curriculum action plan

67. When developing counseling programs, what type of outcomes are associated with success?

a. Counselor-activity outcomes
b. Community involvement outcomes
c. Parent involvement outcomes
d. Student outcomes

68. Which of the following correctly describes the concept of validity as it relates to standardized tests?

a. A valid test score accurately reflects the number of questions answered correctly.
b. If a test is reliable, it is almost always valid.
c. If a test is valid, then it measures what it was intended to measure.
d. A valid test is one that is approved to fulfill federal testing requirements.

69. A counselor develops a peer-mentoring program. What is the main responsibility of the counselor during the implementation of this program?

a. Overseeing all actions of the peer mentors
b. Training peer mentors in various counseling aspects
c. Meeting with mentees to make sure the mentors are doing their jobs
d. Monitoring progress and supporting the peer mentors

70. A local plant recently closed down, causing hundreds of adults in your community to lose their jobs. How might this affect the school district's community?

a. Schools may experience a drop in attendance and achievement.
b. Students will be able to spend more time with their parents and, as a result, do better in school.
c. The number of students in schools will decrease as families move to find work.
d. There may be an increase in participation in the school's on-the-job training program, as students need to work to help the family financially.

71. What forms can professional development take?

a. Continued education
b. Evaluating and reporting on program outcomes
c. Presenting research at professional conferences
d. All of the above

72. Counselors have a professional responsibility to provide parents with what type of information?

a. The details of sessions with their children
b. Objective reports with respect to ethical guidelines
c. Subjective reports on their child's progress
d. Positive parenting information

73. Ms. Taylor is a school counselor who is working with a family that is new to her school. The children do not have documents such as social security cards and Ms. Taylor suspects that the children are undocumented immigrants. What is Ms. Taylor's ethical obligation regarding her students' rights in this situation?

a. Ms. Taylor should call her local immigration office to report the family's undocumented status.
b. Ms. Taylor should refer the family to an immigration attorney to help them seek legal status.
c. Ms. Taylor should ensure that the students' records accurately reflect their immigration status.
d. Ms. Taylor should advocate for the students to have equal access to all school programs.

74. One major risk factor for students is having parents with little or no education or parents who do not speak English as a first language. As a counselor, how could you address this issue?

a. Offer educational opportunities for parents, such as reading and writing classes.
b. Suggest to parents that they enroll in college and earn degrees.
c. Develop educational programs that teach students to be independent of their families.
d. Provide counseling services to all students who have uneducated parents.

Refer to the following for question 75:

> A counselor currently works in a school with a traditional counseling program that offers crisis counseling in times of need. Additionally, due to a lack of support programs, students who get into fights are often sent to the crisis-counseling program. After witnessing a number of students repeatedly getting into fights, a counselor sees that many fights are due to communication problems and simple misunderstandings, and the school's traditional counseling program is having little effect on students involved in fights. As a result, the counselor decides to change the current counseling model to a developmental counseling program.

75. In developing the new programs, the counselor decides to address essential skills with the students. What specific skills does he want to address?

a. Developmental skills
b. Social literacy skills
c. Cognitive skills
d. Emotional literacy skills

76. Which of the following activities within an ASCA National Model program allows a school counselor to demonstrate a leadership role?

a. Define and share counseling program mission and vision statements.
b. Refer students to community agencies for mental health counseling.
c. Participate as part of an IEP team for a student with a learning disability.
d. Create an advisory council and discuss program outcomes.

77. Teachers need basic safety training in school violence to learn how to keep themselves and students safe. In addition to this basic safety training, what other issues should be discussed to assist teachers in understanding problems in their schools?

a. Student dynamics
b. Basic psychology of the student involved in violence
c. Nonviolent reactions to student behavior
d. All of the above

78. The requirement for school counseling program evaluations and school counseling program accountability is discussed in all of the following documents EXCEPT:

a. The ASCA National Model
b. ASCA Ethical Standards for School Counselors
c. ASCA Mindsets & Behaviors for Student Success
d. ASCA School Counselor Professional Standards & Competencies

79. A school counselor implements a classroom guidance program aimed at improving graduation rates. During the annual program evaluation, the counselor analyzes a variety of data to determine the effectiveness of the program and implement changes for the following year. Which of the following pieces of data gathered by the counselor represents perception data?

a. 450 students in grades 9-12 completed three classroom lessons with their counselor.
b. 120 9th-grade students submitted complete four-year graduation plans to their counselor.
c. 135 students indicated they feel "very prepared" to complete high school in four years.
d. The school's current four-year graduation rate is 83%, an increase of 7% over last year.

80. Which of the following outcome data best indicates the need for program improvement?

a. A student-to-school-counselor ratio of 350:1
b. Counselors spending 20% or less of their time on planning and school support services
c. A reduction of 10% or less in discipline referrals
d. Counselors spending 80% or more of their time on direct and indirect services

Answer Key and Explanations for Test #2

1. C: As with most solution-focused brief counseling, the process of termination is guided by the client's understanding of their own goal and picturing their desired outcomes. Asking the client how they will know when they are done with their counseling sessions allows the client to visualize their desired outcome and articulate the specifics of their goal. While there is not a limit to the number of sessions in this type of therapy, the number of sessions is typically limited because clients make progress quickly. Goal progress and readiness for termination are measured by the client's perception, not the counselor's observation. The client may not have completely met their goal by the time they are ready to terminate their counseling sessions, but rather may have made a great deal of progress toward that goal and feel confident in their ability to continue to make progress.

2. B: Almost all parents believe that they have well-behaved, intelligent children; therefore, some parents are quick to become defensive and unwilling to listen when schools call regarding problems with their children. As a counselor, it often falls on you to set up parent conferences. It is important to keep in mind the feelings and beliefs of the parents as well as the policies of the school. By speaking to parents with openness and allowing them to be a part of decision-making processes, the counselor allows a partnership to develop. By creating this sense of partnership and cooperation, the counselor keeps the student's best interests in focus.

3. A: A focus on external punishment or consequences rather than concepts of morality is typical of seven-year-old children and is described by Kohlberg's "obedience and punishment" stage of development. The child's comment indicates the desire to avoid punishment as the main motivator for moral behavior. According to Kohlberg, most children under the age of nine are in stage 1 or stage 2 of moral development.

4. B: School counselor is not a section within the Assess component of the ASCA National Model. The Assess component focuses on evaluating program effectiveness through tools such as Annual Results Reports and measures of student impact, not on role descriptors. These sections are used to analyze how students are affected by the school counseling program. In contrast, school counselor refers to a role within the program, not a component or section used for assessment. Therefore, B is the correct answer.

5. B: ASCA has a large body of research, including topics such as counseling theory and techniques, effectiveness of counseling programs, and the ASCA National Model. Counselors can utilize the thorough research published by ASCA to support their advocacy efforts, including the recommended student-to-counselor ratio of 250:1. School counselors can support their request at their own school or district level using their individual program data (such as the use-of-time assessment, annual calendar, or Recognized ASCA Model Program application) but are likely to find that nationwide, peer-reviewed data is more effectively leveraged in their efforts.

6. D: A school counselor's skills in individual and small group counseling can certainly be a benefit to students with disabilities. However, as with all students, providing long-term individual counseling is out of the scope of appropriate responsibilities. By providing long-term individual counseling for students with IEPs, the counselor would be working outside of the scope of their training and expertise. In addition, providing this type of service to students with IEPs could lead to the school counselor only having time to provide IEP services, leaving general education students without access to the school counseling program.

7. A: In this situation, Mrs. Johnson was primarily advocating for her student's legal rights under Section 504. Typically, the leadership role applies to the development and delivery of a comprehensive school counseling program, while the consultant role usually involves a third party. Convening a team meeting may involve collaboration, but the counselor's role in this scenario was as an advocate for the rights of her student.

8. A: A reinforcement is a consequence that increases the likelihood of the target behavior happening again. Reinforcements can be positive or negative. Positive reinforcements reward the target behavior with something pleasant or enjoyable, while negative reinforcements reward the target behavior with the removal of something unpleasant or undesirable. B.F. Skinner's famous experiment involved rats who pushed a lever to escape a painful electric current, which was a negative reinforcement. Punishment is the opposite of reinforcement, as it decreases the likelihood of the behavior happening again. Neutral consequences do not affect the frequency of the target behavior.

9. C: The laissez-faire group leader generally has little participation or provides little guidance to the group; group members are generally able to make their own decisions without leader interference. Groups led by laissez-faire group leaders have a tendency to be less productive. Autocratic and authoritarian are actually two different terms for the same type of leadership style; autocratic leaders are more likely to give orders or direction to the group and expect group members to comply. Group members typically prefer this style the least. Finally, democratic leaders do provide direction and guidance for group members, but they balance that with participation in the group and input from group members. In most situations, the democratic leadership style is preferred and leads to the best outcomes for the group.

10. B: Standardized tests are a common experience and data point for schools across the country, and many schools and districts have used the results of these tests in all of the ways described in the answer choices. However, ASCA warns against placing too strong of an emphasis on individual test scores. Standardized tests provide only one data point in making decisions about curriculum, instruction, and the education of individual students. School counselors advocate for the use of multiple measures of student progress in making decisions about advanced or remedial coursework, intervention services, promotion, and retention. School counselors also advocate for the use of multiple measures in guiding school improvement, curriculum development, or instructional coaching. Standardized test scores can provide valuable information about academic achievement or school improvement, especially when the data is disaggregated by subgroup or compared to a norm-referenced group. However, this data should not be the sole or even primary data point in making decisions about students.

11. C: In this example, the school counselor is seeking information from the speech therapist, the expert in stuttering. This is an example of consultation performed to benefit a student. Each of the other examples listed is an example of collaboration.

12. D: The School Data Summary Template can be used in conjunction with the school's Student Information System (SIS) to identify and track trends among student subgroups. An SIS provides useful data for a student's achievement, attendance, and discipline. This data can be entered and tracked on the School Data Summary Template to determine which students may need more support and how the school counseling program can become more efficient and effective. The ASCA SMART Goal Template collects information on a targeted subgroup and specifies the percentage of change estimated from baseline outcome measures. The ASCA Fourth Edition National Model (2019) replaced the Third Edition's Excel chart reporting of disaggregated data over time with the

School Data Summary Template. The School Data Summary Template is not used to organize individualized student improvement plans.

13. D: The ASCA Ethical Standards for School Counselors indicate that counselors have a duty to refer when students need a higher level of support than a counselor can adequately provide. In making referrals, counselors should be careful not to endorse any specific provider and, when possible, should provide parents with a vetted list of possible counselors that is approved by the district. The duty to refer does not apply to counselors who feel that they cannot provide services to a student based on their personal or religious beliefs; in those scenarios, counselors should seek additional training and development.

14. A: Under FERPA, students do not become "eligible students" who are granted access to their educational records until they are 18 years old or attending a post-secondary institution. Therefore, a 16-year-old would need their parents to request access to their records. Parents are permitted to inspect or request items be removed from their child's educational record at any time; even if the parent does not have physical custody of the child, they are permitted access to educational records unless a court order states otherwise. Schools are permitted to create a directory of student contact information as long as parents are given "reasonable time" to opt out of sharing directory information.

15. C: Special education evaluations should be comprehensive evaluations that utilize a variety of data from multiple sources. End-of-grade standardized test scores should never be the sole data point to qualify or disqualify a child from receiving special education services.

16. B: The school counselor's first step in completing the ASCA Fourth Edition Annual Administrative Conference Template is to provide findings from the School Data Summary. The School Data Summary identifies data priorities, which then become the means for addressing annual student outcome goals. Other areas of ASCA's Annual Administrative Conference Template include school counselor use of time, student-to-counselor ratio, program implementation plan, and school and district committees and professional work.

17. B: Problem-centered, structured counseling groups allow students to share their experiences and hear similar experiences from their peers in a safe environment. This type of group setting also allows students to gain the support of their peers and receive feedback. Counselors conducting these groups should focus on changing deviant behaviors and encouraging participants to try out new behaviors during the week. These exercises can be discussed during sessions, and students can learn how to brainstorm appropriate behaviors together by sharing their experiences. While it is possible to conduct a problem-centered group for a number of different issues, topics such as self-actualization, safety, and physiological issues are typically the focus of primary prevention groups.

18. D: People often confuse "collaborative" and "compromising" solutions as the same type of solution, but they are different. Collaborative solutions are usually considered the ideal outcome of conflict resolution processes. In a collaborative solution, each party has their needs met and is satisfied with the outcome; this is also thought of as a "win-win" solution. Answer choice C would be a compromise solution, where each party gives up something they want in order to appease the other. A compromise may keep the peace on the surface, but oftentimes one or both parties are at least partially unsatisfied with the outcome. Both answer choices A and B describe accommodating styles, where one party acquiesces to the needs of the other.

19. C: There are a number of professional associations available for counselors to participate in at the local, state, and national levels. For example, the American School Counselor Association is a national organization made up of professionals from various backgrounds, from child development to clinical training. These associations provide professionals with current information on counseling practices, opportunities to attend conferences, and continued education. Additionally, professional associations offer a network of other professionals who are available to discuss counseling strategies and other issues a counselor may face. Counselors must keep in mind the ethical practices of sharing confidential information with colleagues.

20. D: If an assessment is valid, it will not matter what time of day it is given. The assessment will still measure what it was intended to measure. Each of the other choices, however, may impact the ability of the test to measure what it was intended to measure. For example, altering the length of time or number of test items may allow the test-taker to complete more of the test or prevent them from completing the test. These conditions could alter the individual's score simply based on time rather than their achievement level. Explaining a test question, especially on a reading test, could impact the validity of those questions that were explained in different terms, especially if the terms in the original question were part of what was being assessed.

21. D: In any circumstance where a student requires long-term individual counseling or has significant mental health concerns beyond the scope of the school counselor's training, working with the parent (and student, if appropriate) to seek an outside mental health referral is appropriate. School counselors should not provide long-term mental health counseling in a school setting. Because nothing indicates a risk of crisis, an immediate crisis evaluation without parental permission would not be appropriate. While webinars for professional development and consultation with fellow professionals could help the counselor support the student in school, ultimately an outside referral is most appropriate for this situation due to the suspected mental health concern and need for long-term counseling.

22. A: Annual surveys are an easy and effective way to learn about the level of participation, interests, and abilities of parents. These surveys can be sent to parents at the beginning of the year and offer parents the opportunity to volunteer for long- or short-term projects. Surveys should include information about the parents' willingness to participate, their availability, and any special skills they may have. A preliminary list of volunteer events or projects should also be included in these surveys so that parents can select opportunities that correspond with their schedules and interests. By reaching beyond the PTA for support and assistance, schools will develop lasting partnerships with parents and improve the learning environment for the students.

23. C: The use-of-time assessment is a document that helps school counselors determine how much of their time is spent in each of the components of the ASCA National Model, including the breakdown of direct and indirect services. The ideal breakdown of time is 80% spent on direct and indirect student services, while the remaining 20% goes to school support and program management. While many school counselors could estimate their use of time and enter that information into a survey or Excel spreadsheet, a calendar such as Google Calendar would be more likely to help counselors accurately calculate their use of time. The school's student information system may have helpful information about student use of time or fair-share duties, depending on how the school uses the program, but this would not be as useful as the digital calendar. Sick time documentation would not help counselors determine how they are using the time they are at school.

24. B: Pre- and post-test data measures what participants know, believe, or can do. In this case, the pre- and post-test data specifically measures the competencies targeted during the intervention, so it would be likely to measure the effectiveness of the closing-the-gap action plan. Student surveys are another way to collect perception data, but closing-the-gap action plans specifically target a group or demographic of students, so the surveys of the whole school would not be helpful in evaluating a closing-the-gap action plan unless the data was disaggregated by subgroup. Sign-in sheets would be a method of collecting process data, and collecting this information at each portion of the intervention (such as each parent night, small group session, classroom guidance lesson, etc.) would identify data about the action plan specifically. Academic data, such as grades or achievement test results, could be an appropriate method of measuring outcome data related to an action plan, but unless the data is disaggregated by subgroup, it would not be useful in evaluating the effectiveness of the action plan.

25. B: According to ASCA, the counselor has an ethical obligation to tell the principal that teaching the class puts students at potential risk because the counselor may be called away to assist with a crisis, which would leave the class unsupervised and place them at risk. Additionally, grading leads to a dual relationship and should be avoided.

26. D: Social bullying is bullying that focuses on damaging or reducing a victim's social relationships, including exclusion or spreading rumors. Social bullying is most common in female students. While middle school boys are more likely to experience or participate in physical bullying, such as hitting, kicking, or fighting, they are not immune to social bullying. Cyberbullying can be a form of social or verbal bullying, including name-calling, spreading rumors, making threats, exclusion, and other types of harassment; cyberbullying is common at the middle school level. Finally, many bullying prevention programs identify various roles students play in bullying, including the role of "bystander" or "onlooker," a student who witnesses bullying but does nothing to stop the bully or support the victim; a student in this role is considered to be supporting the bullying behavior.

27. D: A diagnostic assessment for learning needs focuses on four main factors: prior knowledge, misconceptions, interests, and learning style preferences. The purpose of this type of assessment is to determine the student's strengths and weaknesses in order to develop an effective intervention strategy. Diagnostic assessments can be done in either formal or informal settings and in either individual or group settings. In the case of a formal setting, counselors can conduct a student survey or skills test. For informal settings, the counselor can simply ask a student or groups of students various questions pertaining to each factor. For example, a counselor may ask, "Do you like to learn by reading a book or seeing material presented in picture form?"

28. A: The define component contains these standards. The define component of the ASCA National Model seeks to define school counseling as a profession and sets the parameters for quality school counseling programs. The manage component of the model aims to provide school counselors with the frameworks and tools they need to make their school counseling program successful. The deliver component of the model helps school counselors provide appropriate services to their students, directly or indirectly, in order to improve student achievement and behavior. The assess component of the model encourages school counselors to regularly assess their school counseling activities to ensure they are effective.

29. C: For comprehensive school counseling programs to be effective and efficient, they must be integrated into the total educational process. This is accomplished by delivering programs that improve shared outcomes. These data-driven measures allow counselors to serve clearly delineated duties, roles, and responsibilities, ensuring that all students have equitable access to services. Serving on leadership teams is not as effective as focusing on demonstrable outcomes. Sharing administrative duties takes the counselor away from their responsibilities, and collaborating on school-wide initiatives may also blur the counselor's role, resulting in a disjointed school counseling program.

30. B: There are three types of action plans that can be created as part of a comprehensive school counseling program: curriculum action plan, small-group action plan, and closing-the-gap action plan. Therefore, the three corresponding results reports to analyze the effectiveness of these action plans are the curriculum results report, small-group results report, and closing-the-gap results report. There is not an individual counseling action plan or results report.

31. C: Based on this one data point, targeted intervention for 7th-grade students is the most appropriate option. If an entire grade level is lagging behind others in terms of attendance rates, a small group intervention does not target the group of students whose outcome data is lagging. Choices A and D could be important additional perception data points in designing an intervention, but they are not interventions in themselves.

32. B: Although counselors have a responsibility to their clients, they are also ethically accountable for the safety of others; this must be disclosed at the beginning of a counseling relationship. If a client ever threatens to harm themselves or someone or something else, the rules of confidentiality do not apply. It is up to the counselor to make a professional judgment about any threatening statements a client might make to determine if alerting authorities and breaking confidentiality is necessary. Many counselors will consult with another professional if a situation is ambiguous. After determining the validity of a threat to do harm, counselors must inform their clients of their intent to notify the proper authorities.

33. C: Consultation is an indirect service conducted on behalf of the student for the student's benefit, while individual student planning and responsive services are both examples of direct services provided directly to the student. Creating an action plan is an ASCA National Model tool based on schoolwide or subgroup data that does not involve an individual student.

34. D: A stanine score of 6 means that the student scored in the 60th to 76th percentile. In a normed achievement test, raw scores are fit to a bell-shaped curve, which can be used to determine percentile ranking. A stanine is a means for scaling scores on a nine-point scale, with a mean of five and a standard deviation of two. Approximately 17% of test takers earn a stanine of 6. The raw score is unaltered data representing the number of correct items for the reading subtest. The grade-equivalent score is the median score for that grade level.

35. A: The recommended and most commonly used practice for academic intervention plans is a strengths-based focus. Most students needing an academic intervention plan are already aware (or their parents and teachers are aware) of the problems they are facing. The school counselor's role in the academic intervention process is to identify the strengths the student has that may be supported in order to increase academic outcomes. The interventions designed in this type of plan are typically focused on either utilizing existing strengths or overcoming barriers. Cognitive behavioral therapy describes a method of one-on-one counseling, which at times may be a part of the plan, but it would not be the approach used to actually develop the plan. Family factors are often considered in developing academic intervention plans, but family therapy is not part of a school counselor's duties and should not be used to develop an academic intervention plan.

36. D: Developmental guidance programs offer schools a full-service guidance program. These programs take all factors of a student's life into consideration: academics, developmental growth, social skills, and emotional maturity. By focusing on developmental stages as well as positive self-esteem, counselors can assist students in reaching their full potential as human beings rather than succeeding only academically. When creating this type of guidance program, counselors are aware of human development in various aspects, including social, emotional, and cognitive growth and development. Developmental guidance programs often rely on the support and participation of the school, families, and communities in order to offer students support and opportunities for learning and personal growth.

37. C: The primary purpose of assessing a comprehensive school counseling program (CSCP) is to analyze progress toward its successful implementation. The ASCA National Model serves as a framework for creating a CSCP; it includes the four components of Define, Manage, Deliver, and Assess in academic, social/emotional, and career domains. The Define component includes establishing student and professional standards (e.g., ASCA Mindsets and Behaviors for Student Success). Manage relates to planning, organizing, and implementing aspects of the CSCP (e.g., program focus, program planning). Deliver refers to direct (e.g., classroom instruction) and indirect (e.g., collaboration with stakeholders) services.

38. C: Programs addressing teen pregnancy are designed to offer students education and support for various issues. As a counselor, regardless of your personal beliefs, you must be sensitive to the needs and views of your students. Prevention programs can provide education about safe sex, as well as information about the reality of being pregnant and being a teenage parent. These prevention programs should be geared toward those who are not pregnant, but who may currently be (or be thinking about) being sexually active. Intervention programs should be geared toward those who are currently pregnant or recently had a child. These programs should provide supportive services along with education about being a teenage parent. Whenever possible, involving the student's parents in the programs will help increase the student's support system.

39. D: Counseling is a direct student service, while consulting, collaborating, and evaluating are all indirect services. Specifically, counseling is a responsive, direct service. Consultation and collaboration can be easily confused for direct services because they involve working directly with other professionals or stakeholders, often in "direct" response to a student need. However, direct services are defined as services provided to students.

40. D: Regardless of the type of abuse a girl may experience, there will be deep psychological effects that may last much longer than the actual abuse. Often, these girls will have low self-esteem and look for ways to make themselves feel better. Additionally, those children who are abused may turn to drugs and alcohol to numb the effects of the abuse. Teenage girls who experience abuse are also more likely to become pregnant than those girls who do not experience abuse. Finally, those experiencing abuse will often lose interest in school and their futures, and counselors will see a decline in their grades. Since the idea of abuse is often thought of as taboo and embarrassing, counselors should be aware of these risk factors and outcomes when assessing students.

41. B: An educational group is one that is designed to teach information and develop skills, regardless of the topic. Therefore, a group that teaches parenting skills would be considered an educational group. A group that focuses on processing a common experience of grief and loss would be an example of a support group, while the group planning a school event would be a task group. Finally, the group focused on overcoming test anxiety would be considered a counseling or therapy group.

42. D: Consultation is an important role for school counselors in supporting student achievement, advocating for students, and understanding student needs. Because consultation is not directly working with the student, it is considered an indirect service. Responsive services (such as counseling and crisis response), individual student planning (appraisal and advisement), and school counseling core curriculum (small group counseling, classroom guidance) are all direct student services.

43. D: Often, schools get into the habit of holding meetings at the same times year after year. In the case of parent-teacher conferences, which are often held during the day, working parents may have to take off work to attend. Additionally, many school council and PTA meetings are held in the evening. While this may be more convenient for working parents, busy families often find it difficult to participate in these events. By offering various times and days for these meetings and events, a school can maximize the participation of the parents.

44. D: Program evaluations are essential for guidance counseling programs. These evaluations will provide information on the effectiveness of a program and allow the counselor to make adjustments and improvements to these programs as necessary. When beginning an evaluation, the counselor should compile various forms of documentation about the program. This will include curriculum guides, unit lesson plans, and the school's master schedule for the counseling programs. This information will help give the counselor a picture of the school's current programs, which will allow the counselor to determine if the guidance curriculum is meeting the students' academic, emotional, and social needs.

45. C: Making a gentle connection between group members is an appropriate strategy to draw out a quiet group member; this skill is known as "linking." Ignoring the fact that James is not participating in the group is not appropriate, as other group members may begin to focus on James's non-participation by trying to draw him out or by becoming withdrawn themselves. Pulling an individual group member aside during a group session is typically not appropriate, as it takes the focus away from the group's collective focus, and removing a member from the group can shake the trust of the remaining group members.

46. C: Counselors must be careful when conducting training programs involving parents. Parents may be sensitive and misinterpret these trainings as the school trying to change their core values and methods in raising their children. Schools can offer other types of support to increase parent involvement. Some suggestions include providing parents with information on effective study skills, recommending time limits for homework, or babysitting during PTA meetings and parent-teacher conferences. The goal of offering parents these various services is to increase participation and develop strong parent support for the school. Counselors should also keep in mind that parents do not necessarily have to be at the school to be active with the school. When parents help their children with homework or participate in a phone tree, they are offering much-needed support.

47. A: IDEA, the Individuals with Disabilities Education Act, provides for the education of children with disabilities by requiring schools to provide a free appropriate public education through an individualized education plan (IEP) to children with disabilities in one of thirteen categories. These categories are: autism, deaf-blindness, developmental delay, emotional disturbance, hearing impairments (including deafness), intellectual disability, multiple disabilities, orthopedic impairments, other health impairments, specific learning disabilities, speech or language impairments, traumatic brain injury, and visual impairments (including blindness). Therefore, the school counselor would refer to the provisions of this law as well as school policies under IDEA to provide information to Hanna's parents. The other laws named in answer choices are Section 504, the Family Educational Rights and Privacy Act (FERPA), and the Every Student Succeeds Act (ESSA). Section 504 is also a disability-related law, but Section 504 addresses how a school will provide accommodations and modifications to remove the barriers a child's disability may create for accessing the curriculum; an IEP outlines a specific educational plan including specialized instruction. FERPA has to do with the privacy of student records, and ESSA is a federal law guiding K-12 public education policy.

48. A: Elementary school is the time when children are learning the most and developing important motor skills and mental functions. Counselors must be able to recognize developmental delays, as well as advanced learners. School counselors will be major advocates for students who may experience developmental delays. While the other options may be important, these issues are more likely seen at the junior high and high school levels. Knowledge in continued education will be important for high school students who wish to pursue a college education; counselors with students in these age groups will need to educate students and offer assistance in applying to colleges and obtaining financial aid and scholarships. Additionally, relationship building, adjustment, and coping mechanisms are issues most often seen in junior high school, as these years are a time of many changes physically, emotionally, and educationally.

49. A: Generally speaking, the mean is less than the median in distributions with data skewed to the left. The mean, median, and mode (i.e., measures of central tendency) are all the same values in a normal distribution. In distributions skewed right (i.e., positive distributions), the mode is less than the median, and the median is less than the mean.

50. A: Many of the communication and active listening techniques employed by peer mediation programs to resolve student conflicts are the same types of techniques and skills used by counselors in individual counseling. "I think you should..." is a phrase that implies giving advice, which is not productive in a peer mediation process (or in individual counseling). Peer mediation programs focus on training students to facilitate collaboration between peers, not resolve their conflicts for them. "Can you tell me more?" is a probing question, "What I hear you saying is..." is a paraphrase, and "I can see why you feel that way" is a validating statement; all of these are appropriate and helpful techniques in peer mediation.

51. B: The best rationale for assessing the program is to determine if any improvements need to be made. Stakeholders are invested in the program's success, which means that looking for areas for improvement is a sound reason for performing an assessment. The ASCA National Model provides a framework for defining, managing, delivering, and assessing school programs targeting all students. The rationale for assessing the program is to ensure that the program is informed by data for all students (Tier 1) rather than only subsets of students (Tier 2 and Tier 3). The school district does not mandate that school counselors perform the assessment.

52. B: Mentor-mentee programs are a well-researched intervention for students at-risk. Tier I interventions are school-wide programs designed to provide quality instruction and support for all students. "At-risk" students, such as those who are failing courses, have chronic absenteeism, were retained in the previous grade level, or have various other risk factors would most likely require a tier II or tier III intervention, typically in a small group or one-on-one setting. Therefore, a mentor-mentee program designed for at-risk students would not be a tier I intervention. Research supports mentor-mentee programs as having positive impacts on student outcomes, both academic and behavioral. Mentor-mentee programs can be found both in the community and within schools. School counselors wishing to implement mentor-mentee programs could design and manage their own program or seek out a community resource for their students; regardless of where the program is managed, counselors should ensure parent permission for students to participate, especially when volunteers from the community are serving as mentors or when mentors may seek information about their mentees' progress in school.

53. B: Analyzing a results report is part of the Assess component of the ASCA National Model, not the Manage component. Results reports are used to evaluate the effectiveness of classroom instruction, small-group services to students, and closing-the-gap action plans. Completing a use-of-time assessment, creating a closing-the-gap action plan, and writing a mission and vision statement are all part of the effective management of a comprehensive school counseling program. These activities help counselors clarify the needs of their school and students and define priorities for their program.

54. D: A well-designed needs assessment can be a powerful tool for school counselors in identifying areas of need, defining goals, and planning programming. Needs assessments can also identify areas where there may be equity gaps, individual student concerns, or common student concerns that may be addressed by small-group counseling. While it may be tempting to use a needs assessment to track changes in data from year to year as a form of program evaluation, this is not the purpose for which they are designed, and they are unlikely to be effective for program evaluation due to changes in student enrollment or staffing from year to year and a lack of specificity within the questions to evaluate individual programs.

55. C: The Deliver component of the comprehensive school counseling program includes all types of direct and indirect services, which ideally make up 80% or more of a counselor's time. The Deliver component includes instruction, appraisal and advisement, and counseling; these services are delivered through individual counseling, small groups, and classroom lessons.

56. A: Advising a colleague on reporting suspected cases of child abuse is an example of consultation. Consultation involves seeking, providing, or receiving information, recommendations, opinions, or expertise for a student's academic, career, and social/emotional needs. Activities that characterize collaboration include, but are not limited to, helping a teacher develop grade-appropriate classroom rules, serving as district representative on career development committees, and providing ongoing teacher training on how to recognize mental health warning signs. Consultation can be collaborative, but it differs from collaboration in that consultation generally involves the counselor taking actionable steps on behalf of the student to meet a common goal.

57. A: Assertiveness training groups are typically highly structured and focus on practicing skills learned in the group through role-playing. Linking and encouraging may be used in many types of groups, so it is not specific to an assertiveness training cognitive behavioral therapy (CBT) group. The empty chair technique could be used in assertiveness training, but it is a Gestalt technique, not a CBT technique.

58. A: Beginning a solution-focused brief counseling session involves having the student define the problem and determine their desired goals for the counseling. With the assistance of the counselor, the intervention or behavior change is both determined and initiated by the student. Strategic tasks are assigned by the counselor and involve a direct behavior change. For example, if a student is having difficulty with academics and has a goal to raise his grades, then a strategic task would be for him to study for one hour every night. In subsequent counseling sessions, the counselor would offer support and positive feedback in order to encourage the student to reach his academic goals. Once the goals for that particular problem have been reached, the sessions are no longer required, and counseling is terminated.

59. D: One major benefit of ASCA membership, even for school counseling students, is the availability of professional liability insurance. University field experiences offices or local school districts may add interns to their policies, but this varies widely. ASCA is the best option for Mr. Dean. The National Board for Certified Counselors is not an option for school counseling students who have not yet earned their degree.

60. B: Proper delegation of responsibilities will lead to more effective counseling programs. There are many opportunities for teachers and students to participate in leading programs. For example, developing a teacher advisor program increases participation from teachers and offers students a larger support system. Peer mentoring programs allow mentors the ability to increase their leadership skills and allow mentees the opportunity to widen their network of support systems. Counselors who encourage the assistance of teachers and students with various programs will foster a cohesive school that works together toward a common goal. This cohesiveness will provide all students with the best possible learning environment.

61. B: Pavlov's theory of conditioning responses states that when an action is repeatedly followed by a response, the one performing the action will either continue or stop doing so, depending on the response. In this case, the child continually receives a negative response from his peers. Theoretically, the child would begin to relate his actions to this negative response and cease the action. However, this is not occurring and may be an indication of developmental delays. As seen in the vignette, the child has little social support at home, and there is a clear indication of other interpersonal issues with his parents. To help this child, a counselor could explore social development delays he has and propose some type of intervention.

62. A: Norm-referenced tests compare an individual's test score to those of a comparison group, typically a group of same-age or same-grade peers. For many state-standardized tests, a child's individual score is compared to a norm group of students across the state, and sometimes there are additional norm groups for the school or district. Parents who are trying to understand their child's test scores may confuse a percentile rank with a percentage of correct answers on the test itself, but they are very different data points. Norm-referenced tests compare an individual's performance to a comparison group, while criterion-referenced tests compare an individual's performance to a set of standards or objectives to be mastered. End-of-grade tests often do measure a student's mastery of grade-level standards, but the indication that this child's test score is from a "norm-referenced" test means that their results are calculated in comparison with their peers.

63. B: School counselors provide direct services to students with serious emotional disturbances through community advocacy. Several administrative or supervisory activities fall outside the purview of the school counselor, including supervising individualized education program (IEP) implementation or writing 504 and IEP plans. Additionally, school counselors provide short-term rather than long-term counseling and support.

64. A: This example most directly demonstrates the idea of "installation of hope," whereby group members can see others' successes and feel hopeful about their own prospects for growth and improvement. The concept of universality describes the understanding that what group members are experiencing is not unusual and they are not alone in their experiences. Group cohesiveness explains the sense of belonging that group members feel when working toward a common group goal. "Imparting information" could be a tricky answer choice in this scenario. Jim is sharing his experience with the group, but he is not necessarily sharing new information that they could learn from. "Installation of hope" is a better fit for this situation because the information Jim shared could inspire other group members in their progress.

65. C: Cultural bias is a potentially significant problem affecting the validity of tests and should be considered not only when selecting and administering tests but also when interpreting test results. Cultural bias occurs when differences in test-takers' gender, race, ethnicity, or socioeconomic status impact their background knowledge, understanding of test items, or understanding of the behaviors required to successfully complete a test. For example, a test that includes an English idiom in a math question may not be accessible for English language learners, and their success on that test item could be affected due to their English proficiency, rather than their math ability. A test item asking students to complete a phrase from a nursery rhyme may not be accessible to students

...does not practice or sing that nursery rhyme, or a reading passage that ...polo may be confusing for students who do not have background knowledge related to ...due to their socioeconomic status or culture. Differences in classroom groupings would not result in a cultural bias, but they could result in a difference in instructional quality or curriculum taught, which could affect student outcomes on tests.

66. A: The annual calendar identifies the major activities of the school counseling program and publishes them in a manner that is accessible to stakeholders. The annual calendar can be used by the school counselor to increase the visibility of their comprehensive school counseling program and help stakeholders understand the components of the program. Activities include classroom guidance lessons, parent nights, student or class meeting dates, standardized test dates, college information meetings or application deadlines, and family activities.

The annual agreement is an ASCA National Model document that is used to outline the school counseling program and establish a formal agreement between the school counselor and school administration regarding counseling program goals. It is typically not a document that stakeholders outside of the counselor and principal have access to. The school data profile is a template used by the school counselor to identify areas of strength and need in their student achievement and behavior data, which can then be used to create action plans or program goals. Finally, a curriculum action plan is a document used by the school counselor to design the classroom guidance program and align the program with curricular goals, but this is not a document that is typically communicated to various stakeholders.

67. D: Ultimately, counseling programs are designed for students. Accordingly, student outcomes will determine the success of a program. As a counselor, it is important to conduct regular evaluation measures on each program offered. These measures will show the success of a program by including information about student improvement and students' ratings of satisfaction with the programs. For example, if a program is intended to improve a student's grades in a math course, outcome measures will include the student's final grades compared to her grades when she began the program. Additionally, conducting student surveys to find out how the students enjoyed the program is beneficial in creating future programs that both engage students and increase their performance.

68. C: Validity refers to a test's ability to measure what it was intended to measure. For example, a state end-of-grade reading assessment is valid if it measures reading standards for that grade level. Reliability, on the other hand, refers to how consistent a test is. That same end-of-grade reading assessment would be reliable if the same student achieved the same results on the test on different days. If a test is valid, it is usually also reliable; however, a test can be reliable without being valid. If an average 3rd grader who takes a college-level reading assessment consistently performs poorly on the assessment, the low score is reliable, but if the test was meant to measure mastery of 3rd-grade reading standards, it would not be valid. Validity does not depend on the number of questions answered correctly or the approval of a test under various laws or testing requirements.

69. D: Peer mentoring programs are beneficial for many students and can address a number of issues. These programs give students the opportunity to guide and lead other students. Counselors spearheading peer mentoring programs are responsible for monitoring the program's overall progress and being available when questions or problems arise, rather than overseeing every action of the peer mentors. Since the focus of these programs is students helping students, micromanagement of peer mentors by a counselor would result in an ineffective and potentially unfulfilling experience for the students. Also, it is not necessary that peer mentors know all aspects of counseling, as their responsibilities in the program will not deal directly with counseling other students. Peer mentors should receive training in leadership and sensitivity to other students' needs.

70. A: Poverty is one of the main risk factors for students. Often, those children who live in poverty do not eat properly or get enough sleep. Some students may be homeless or living with multiple families. Additionally, the strain of a sudden loss of income can cause fighting or tension in the household. As a result, students may not be prepared for school, as they may be too tired or hungry to participate. For a counselor, paying keen attention to the dynamics of a community will be beneficial in assisting students. In this case, the counselor can encourage families to participate in free or reduced-price breakfast or lunch plans at school. Additionally, the counselor can provide families with community resources to assist with financial emergencies.

71. D: Continued education is required for professional licenses. Depending on the state board of education, a counselor will have a specific number of hours in continued education to complete. This education is intended to provide the counselor with the latest counseling information and practices. Additionally, by evaluating and reporting on programs, counselors are able to learn about the success of specific programs as well as areas of improvement. By reporting on the outcomes, counselors are educating the community about the school and its counseling programs. Giving presentations at professional conferences allows the counselor the opportunity to share different counseling practices and strategies with other professionals. The sharing of information promotes professional development and is highly recommended in the counseling profession.

72. B: Students have the right to seek confidential counseling. Counselors should inform parents of this confidentiality, as well as the roles, responsibilities, and expectations of the counselor and the student being counseled. Counselors should also work to provide parents with objective information regarding their children within the scope of confidentiality. At times, it may be necessary to inform the parents of certain issues pertaining to safety. This information will be provided only after the counselor has made a professional judgment that the client is in danger or intends to inflict harm on another and after telling the client of their intention to inform their parents. Finally, the counselor also has a responsibility to keep conversations they have with the parents confidential.

73. D: While immigration is a thorny issue, the Supreme Court ruling *Plyler v. Doe* (1982) is clear in stating that no student, regardless of immigration status, can be prohibited from accessing public K-12 education. Further, the official ASCA Position Statement on this topic states that school counselors have an ethical duty to advocate for equal access to curriculum and services for all students, regardless of immigration status. A comprehensive school counseling program provides academic, social/emotional, and career components for all students.

74. A: As communities become more diverse, counselors are seeing an increase in the number of parents who do not speak English as a first language. Because this dynamic often creates a barrier between these parents and their children's schools, a lack of participation from these parents is common. In these cases, counselors can provide information or opportunities for parents to increase their English skills through free or low-cost programs. Additionally, adult education programs in basic reading, writing, and GED preparation can be offered to parents who wish to increase their skills or earn their GED. Educated parents are able to offer more academic assistance to their children.

75. B: Social literacy skills are also known as interpersonal skills. These skills refer to how individuals relate to one another. The level of these skills also determines an individual's self-esteem, peer acceptance, and self-efficacy. In this situation, it appears that these students are having a difficult time relating to and communicating with each other. A group on crisis intervention will not offer these students the appropriate social skills, as a crisis group is typically geared toward students who are affected by issues such as a death in the family, a natural disaster, or another large crisis. A group that focuses on social literacy skills can help students understand themselves as well as others. This type of group teaches students appropriate social behaviors, communication skills, and techniques for dealing with conflict.

76. A: According to ASCA, defining a program mission and vision statement and publicly sharing those statements with stakeholders is an activity that allows a counselor to demonstrate leadership. In writing these statements, the counselor defines the purpose and direction of the school counseling program and positions the counselor to lead the program toward that vision. Creating an advisory council is an example of collaboration, while referring students to community agencies and serving on IEP teams are examples of collaboration and advocacy.

77. D: Teachers need to understand some of the basic psychology of their students and their students' behaviors. Counselors can help provide teachers with such information in a number of ways, including offering discussion and training sessions throughout the school year. These sessions should provide teachers with a basic understanding of student dynamics and the psychology of student violence. When teachers are aware of these aspects of their students, they will be more aware of what is going on and may be able to respond to issues before a situation escalates to violence. Additionally, teachers need to be aware of their own emotions when dealing with angry or upset students. In order to control a situation that is or may become violent, teachers will need to remain calm and react in nonviolent ways: for example, trying to separate fighting students and talking calmly to them versus pushing a student out of the way and yelling at him.

78. C: The ASCA Mindsets & Behaviors for Student Success does not discuss program evaluations or accountability, although the standards within this document can be utilized by counselors to measure student progress as part of their program evaluation. Each of the other documents explicitly discusses the requirement for counselors to conduct program evaluations. The ASCA National Model includes Accountability as one of its four components and contains a great deal of information about the evaluation process for school counseling programs. The ASCA Ethical Standards for School Counselors contains a section titled "Comprehensive Data-Informed Program" that outlines the purpose for evaluations as well as the ethical considerations in choosing and administering assessments. Finally, within the ASCA School Counselor Professional Standards & Competencies, there is a Behavior category titled "Planning and Assessment," which describes accountability-related behaviors exhibited by effective school counselors.

79. C: With programs aimed at increasing graduation rates, outcome data such as the four-year graduation rate is often the primary piece of data that is highlighted; an effective counselor examines graduation rates even further by disaggregating data into student subgroups in order to identify gaps in achievement. Changes in this rate over time are also important in identifying areas of need or improvements made as a result of school counseling programs. School counselors also impact student mindsets and behaviors through their interventions, and perception data is an important method of measuring how students feel, what they think they know, and what they believe. Answer choice C represents a piece of perception data gathered through a student survey, possibly in a pre- and post-test format, that provides the counselor with information about the effectiveness of their intervention on their students' beliefs. Answer choices A and B represent process data, which is another important type of data to evaluate when evaluating program effectiveness.

80. A: Although national student-to-school-counselor ratios are much higher, ASCA recommends 250:1 to ensure that all students have equitable access to services. School support services (e.g., creating lesson plans, developing classroom action plans) should encompass no more than 20% of a school counselor's time. The remaining time (i.e., 80%) should be spent on direct and indirect services. Unless the school counselor specifies otherwise, a reduction of 10% or less in discipline referrals is not the best indicator of a need for program improvement.